P9-DTS-118

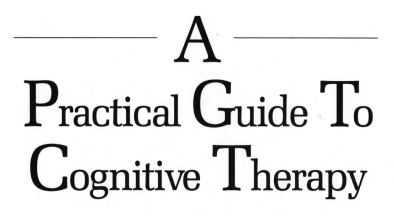

A
Practical Guide To
Cognitive Therapy

Dean Schuyler, M.D.

W • W • NORTON & COMPANY • NEW YORK • LONDON

A NORTON PROFESSIONAL BOOK

By the same author
The Depressive Spectrum

Library of Congress Cataloging-in-Publication Data

Schuyler, Dean, 1942–
A practical guide to cognitive therapy / Dean Schuyler.
p.   cm.
"A Norton professional book."
Includes bibliographical references.
Includes index.
ISBN 0-393-70105-0
1. Cognitive therapy.   I. Title.
[DNLM: 1. Cognitive Therapy — methods.   WM 420 S397p]
RC489.C63S34 1990   616.89'142 – dc20
DNLM/DLC
90-7989

W. W. Norton & Company, Inc., 500 Fifth Avenue, New York, N.Y. 10110
W. W. Norton & Company, Ltd., 10 Coptic Street, London WC1A 1PU

2   3   4   5   6   7   8   9   0

For Ethel

CONTENTS

ACKNOWLEDGMENTS

It is perhaps a measure of the passage of time that the inspiration to write this book came not from my teachers but from my patients and students. My gratitude, however, goes to several important figures in my life whose influence was formative.

One teacher stands above the rest. My mother Ethel provided for me many of the basic beliefs that form the building blocks of my thinking (and my work) today. She established (by herself) a family environment rich in stimulation that I have found difficult to replicate for my children. She taught me respect for the written word and the importance of passing it on to others.

I was born and raised in New York City, where I attended the Bronx High School of Science. Some ideas fundamental to psychotherapy practice were introduced to me at New York University by Phil Zimbardo. An unusually creative and stimulating man, Zimbardo taught "Communication and Attitude Change," which greatly influenced my thinking. Working closely with him on a college honors project derived from cognitive dissonance theory was an unparalleled experience.

Aaron Beck has been my mentor, role model, and friend since we met at the University of Pennsylvania in 1969. The founder of the stream of cognitive therapy that I have practiced for nearly 20 years, Beck continues to provide inspiration in his writings and occasional letters and during those infrequent but important times when we are together.

I spent three years (1971–74) at the National Institute of Mental Health in Rockville, Maryland, working in the areas of suicide and depression research. Here I was introduced to Morris Parloff and began to think seriously for the first time about why psychotherapy worked (when it did).

In 1976, I joined the faculty at Georgetown University School of Medicine, charged with designing a continuing education program. Over the next seven years, I had the opportunity to formulate and teach courses on the cognitive model to psychiatric residents. Dick Steinbach, chairman of the department, was a continuing source of support, encouragement, and confidence. His interest in me provided an anchor when I most needed one. His untimely death in September 1982 was a personal loss.

The unquestioning psychoanalytic environment at Georgetown at that time (1976–83) was inhospitable to the teaching of a different psychotherapeutic system. Some residents were asked by their supervisors to explain their interest in my course in terms of a "resistance to learning how to be a therapist." One group worked hard to combat the obstacles and, as a result, got from me the best I had to give as a teacher. My experience with them was a direct motivator (although with a significant lag time!) for writing this book. I am grateful to this resident group: Dan Levine, Paul Buongiorno, Andy Schiavone, Rich Rosse, Dave Markowitz, Terry Kurtz, John Blankmeier, and Phil Schmitt.

In response to my need at Georgetown for a forum in which to think and talk about the process of psychotherapy, PIG (the Psychotherapy Idea Group) was born in July 1981. Over the next four years this small, elite study group met during work hours at the hospital and then in the evening at members' homes. This changing core of influential thinkers focused their diverse backgrounds, ages, and experiences on the elusive active ingredient question: "When psychotherapy works, why does it work?" Bart Evans, Bob Hedaya, Art Behrmann, and Marsha Chambers were early members. The list of "guest pigs" invited to consider the question with us is a long and distinguished one.

Hedaya, as student, then colleague and friend, has been a continuing influence as we have jointly considered clinically relevant ideas. Edgar Weiss, for 20 years a psychiatric colleague, has been a steadfast friend and has consistently stimulated my clinical thinking.

When the Georgetown department was in turmoil following Steinbach's death. I was engaged by an important teacher I had met at the University of Pennsylvania, Bill Webb. At that time serving as vice president of the Sheppard and Enoch Pratt Hospital in Baltimore, Webb invited me to consult at the hospital as well as to teach and supervise psychiatric residents. I am grateful for his interest and confidence in me and for his encouragement.

Clearly, the psychotherapeutic process is a two-way learning street, especially in a collaborative venture such as cognitive therapy. I have met and interacted with a diverse group of bright, motivated, successful individuals in my practice of adult psychotherapy. I know many of them better than I know my closest social friends. They have given of themselves to me, even when they were feeling needy and dysfunctional. Many of my patients know me as I like to think "I am." To have the opportunity to form relationships in this way is one of the enduring joys of being a psychotherapist.

Stories gathered over the past eighteen years from the lives of my patients can be found throughout the book, To protect their confidentiality, identifying information has been deliberately altered. In some cases, details are compiled from the lives of several people.

My two daughters, Rachel and Amy, are never far from my thoughts. Their antics and approaches to problem–solving have supplied me with a surprising number of clinically relevant tales that I use in my office practice. Terry, my partner in the roller coaster of life, has provoked me, supported me, and often understood more of me than I have of her. I am grateful to my family for their forbearance in support of the writing of this book.

Finally, let me express my gratitude especially to my cognitive colleagues, whose encouragement led directly to this book about what I do: Brian Shaw, John Rush, and Monica Basco.

Although I have been (secretly) working on this book in my mind for a number of years, a large share of the credit for transferring it into print belongs to Susan Barrows of W. W. Norton and Company.

Dean Schuyler
Rockville, Maryland
June, 1990

PREFACE

There have been a number of good books on cognitive therapy: Aaron Beck's *Cognitive Therapy and the Emotional Disorders* (1976), Beck et al.'s *Cognitive Therapy of Depression* (1979), David Burns' *Feeling Good* (1980), Gary Emery et al.'s *New Directions in Cognitive Therapy* (1981), V.F. Guidano and G. Liotti's *Cognitive Processes and Emotional Disorders* (1983), and Rian Mc Mullin's *Handbook of Cognitive Therapy Techniques* (1986) — to name a few. Pioneers of the cognitive model such as Don Meichenbaum and Michael Mahoney, and of the Rational–Emotive Therapy system of Albert Ellis, as well as students of all of the above, have written worthy books. Why do we need another?

Interest among psychiatrists in learning to use this system of psychotherapy is apparently at an all-time high. There were five courses offered covering different aspects of cognitive therapy at the annual meeting of the American Psychiatric Association in Montreal in 1988. All were fully subscribed. Two hundred and four registrants were turned away from my basic course alone. In San Francisco in 1989, an additional two hundred signed up for two renderings of "Cognitive Therapy: The Basics." In New York in May 1990, a repeat of the basic course was again sold out.

At workshops I have been told repeatedly that no book adequately conveys the clinician's experience in "doing" cognitive therapy. Practitioners and students, therefore, take workshops to either start or support the pursuit of learning this model of psychotherapy. It is my hope that this volume will contribute to the cognitive therapy library and to the teaching of this model to clinicians of all backgrounds, as well as to students in the various curricula, and that it will fill the gap by describing the actual clinical experience of doing cognitive therapy on a daily basis.

I believe that learning psychotherapy should begin with a consideration of "what works that therapists do." The opening chapter

considers this issue, in light of the reality that the answers themselves are not yet in. Chapter 2 outlines some practical aspects
inherent to all psychotherapy, preliminary to the presentation of
the cognitive therapy model. The enlarging spectrum of cognitive
therapy's usefulness is considered, along with the prototypical patient for whom it is intended. The course of psychotherapeutic
treatment is traced. Consideration of the implications for programs training psychotherapists of the cognitive model's success
concludes this section.

In Part II, the cognitive model is presented in a conversational,
yet thorough, manner: some background detail, the basic principles of the model, and the techniques derived from the theory.

Part III focuses on applying the model to three circumstances
that occur frequently in clinical practice. These are discussed in
detail as examples of the model at work: the formation and disso-
lution of love relationships, coping with separation and divorce,
and psychotherapy issues with older patients and clients.

In Part IV, the model is extended beyond its original parameters
to form a framework for long-term psychotherapy, to provide a
focus for an approach to reparenting the distressed adolescent, and
to serve as a language in teaching couples to solve marital difficulties. The section's final chapter stresses the usefulness of follow-up
care in psychotherapy in general and within the system of cognitive therapy in particular.

In Part V, the principles and techniques presented earlier are
integrated in three case examples. Although identifying information has been altered in each case to protect the confidentiality of
the patient, the clinical issues are highlighted within the context of
a person's life experience.

As the cognitive model leaves much deliberate room for individual innovation and difference of approach, I don't expect that my
experience will be seen necessarily as typical of all those people
who call themselves cognitive therapists. Rather, I hope that clinicians and students alike will find enough points of contact here to
provoke them to think about the process of psychotherapy in general and the cognitive therapy model in particular.

It must be remembered that there is nothing more difficult to plan, more doubtful of success, nor more dangerous to manage than the creation of a new system. For the initiator has the enmity of all who would profit by the preservation of the old institution and merely lukewarm defenders in those who would gain by the new one.
Machiavelli, The Prince, 1513

Psychotherapy is sought not primarily for enlightenment about the unchangeable past, but because of dissatisfaction with the present and a desire to do better in the future.
Watzlawick, Weakland and Fisch,
Change, 1974

P̶̶̶̶̶̶̶I
Preliminary
Issues

The Active Ingredient Question

1

It was spring 1981. I felt bored, stale, waiting for some stimulation to break the sameness of each day. As a faculty member in the department of psychiatry at Georgetown, I taught the residents the course on affective disorders. I was a cognitive therapist in a world of psychodynamic thinkers. When I began to believe that nothing was likely to present itself, I decided to form PIG.

Brief letters were sent to four other members of the university family asking them to "join an elite group to study the process of psychotherapy." In contrast to the university's emphasis on strict hierarchy and role definition, PIG (Psychotherapy Idea Group) would attempt to stress equal status for its members. A graduating psychiatric resident, a fourth–year and a third–year resident were invited to join the senior members, a psychiatrist and a psychologist. Two were women; three were men. All but one accepted and we began meeting for 90 minutes twice monthly during work hours.

Initially, the sessions were informal and the focus was fixed on "identifying the active ingredients in successful psychotherapy." Whether the group member had seen two patients/clients or had "years of experience," his or her hypotheses were solicited and regarded equally. Most proposals for added structure (e.g., a journal club) were turned down. Articles passed freely among the group, but quoting from the writings of others was often received negatively unless accompanied by a novel idea.

Someone suggested that we invite guests, a kind of "PIG-of-the-Month." For the return of a pastrami sandwich, impressive guests joined our group: Morris Parloff, Leon Salzman, John Wiley, and Loren Mosher were early invitees. Subsequent "Guest PIGs" included Paul Chodoff, Al and Carol Levinthal, Ted Beal, Irene

Elkin, and Barry Wolfe. The question posed to them was always: "When your patients succeed in making changes, what are the active ingredients?"

Shortly after the group's first birthday, we began to meet monthly in the evenings at a member's home. A couple of original members dropped out, some to return subsequently. There were new people added, but the group never exceeded six in number and retained its mix with regard to age, sex, and background. Topics discussed ranged from schizophrenia and obsessive-compulsive personality to cognitive therapy, psychoanalysis, and psychotherapy research. As several of the group were not in the mainstream of the university's psychoanalytic orientation, PIG served to support and encourage dissenting views. Foremost, however, it stimulated a group of clinicians to think about their work as a process separate from considerations of theory.

Mark well that the following does not represent original research. It is instead the result of study group conversation over a four–year period, complemented by active reading of the psychotherapy research literature. Precise assignment of acknowledgment for any original ideas is blurred by the process of the group. Members over the four years were: Dean Schuyler, Bart Evans, Art Behrmann, Bob Hedaya, Marcia Chambers, Ellen Liebenluft, Dan Levine, Diane Arnkoff, Carol Glass, and Morris Parloff.

We began by artificially separating factors into three groupings: those relevant to the therapist, the patient, and the process. We began with three "givens" as fundamental parts of the psychotherapy transaction, as stated by Jerome Frank[1] in 1974: a healer, a sufferer, and a prescribed series of contacts.

THERAPIST VARIABLES

It has been written that the so-called relationship factors (warmth, acceptance, genuineness, empathy) may, by themselves, be the active ingredient in psychotherapeutic change. More likely, they may be necessary but not sufficient. Psychotherapy is a unique transaction, particularly when viewed in the context of medical care. An unwilling sufferer can be given an injection of penicillin to successfully treat a pneumococcal pneumonia. A medical specialist with a gruff and distant "bedside manner" may successfully diagnose and treat an obscure illness. There is, however, no analogy in psychotherapy.

Therefore, the first stage of therapy is often called "engagement." The therapist's task is to "form a bond" with the patient that will facilitate the work they are bound to do. An atmosphere of warmth and acceptance of whatever the patient reveals of him or herself seems related to a positive outcome. In the past decade, the utilization of computers to simulate and deliver psychotherapy threatens the fundamental significance of the relationship factors. Can a distressed individual "form a relationship" with a computer screen? Will the patient "fantasize" a therapist behind or within the computer? Can psychotherapy carried out in this fashion be successful?

In 1974, I role played a suicidal patient to test the "adaptability" of a simple computer program prototype at the University of Wisconsin. I took on the task with great skepticism but in the end felt that the computer had performed impressively well. Computers have not yet nullified the value of the human factor for me in the psychotherapy transaction, but with increasing computer sophistication will therapists someday be rendered obsolete?

A therapist who is genuine, real, and straightforward with his or her patient will usually find engagement an easy task. Psychotherapy consists of a purposeful oscillation between objectivity and comment, on the one hand, and feeling and empathy, on the other. "What the therapist says" can be taught through studying a manual and modeling after a supervisor. "What the therapist feels" may derive from a personality constellation that is difficult to acquire.

It seemed to us in PIG that it would be difficult for a therapist to help a patient he or she could not respect. The issue of "liking" seemed to be important, but not critical. Some of us endorsed the concept that the more nearly alike the therapist and the patient are, the easier it is for them to work together. Others said that there are blind spots where therapist and patient converge. Neither generalization seems warranted. Rather, a working pair that is "on the same wavelength" may have captured the necessary connection to facilitate change. Similarly, an experienced therapist may have an advantage with some patients and a "fresh, un-spoiled" clinician may do better with others.

The polar opposite to the familiar concept of burnout in a therapist is motivation. When the clinician "gets involved" and shows interest, remembers details and demonstrates sensitivity, this requirement is seen to be met. It seems important that the therapist possess and retain a sense of optimism (the expectation that the patient will change). An element underlying self-confidence is the therapist's belief in the validity of his or her approach to psychotherapy.

It has been striking to me that some of my colleagues (who may be highly successful in their psychotherapy practice) can be absolutely tedious in a social setting. I always thought that interpersonal skill was a requisite for success in psychotherapy. Perhaps some "give at the office" and manifest less interest and enthusiasm elsewhere. When the group was challenged to examine skill in communication more closely, the "ability to admit you are wrong" emerged as a useful trait. In addition, the capacity to use fresh, vivid language was seen to be an asset.

The therapist must be able to foster positive expectations in his or her patient. This entails providing encouragement, support, and the stimulus to risk trying something new. The ability to evoke an emotionally charged atmosphere (just enough; not too much) may be an element that fuels change. It was an observation that some clinicians have more tolerance for this element than do others.

The eight therapist variables that may facilitate change in the patient are summarized in Table 1.

PATIENT VARIABLES

Even the "best" of therapists don't help everyone. Conversely, some patients seem likely to succeed in therapy with "almost anyone." Merely seeking help (sometimes just making the decision to do so) is enough to bring the sufferer some relief. He or she has decided to do something constructive about his or her difficulties. He has engaged an expert. He has begun to share a burden by "unburdening himself."

TABLE 1: THERAPIST VARIABLES

1. Relationship factors
   a. Warmth, acceptance, genuineness, empathy
   b. Respect for the patient
   c. Liking the patient
2. Indications that therapist understands patient
3. Motivation
4. Optimism
5. Self-confidence
6. Communication (interpersonal) skill
7. Can provide support, encouragement to try something new
8. Ability to evoke (and tolerate) an emotionally charged atmosphere

It seems important for the patient to generate "hope for change" despite the symptom of hopelessness often encountered in the emotional disorders. The capacity to trust the therapist chosen appears to speed the process of psychotherapy. As a cognitive therapist whose referrals are often specifically for this model, I find that the shared belief in the method utilized seems to facilitate change.

Although psychotherapy has become much more broadly known through magazine articles and television talk shows, some patients still arrive expecting "instant change." The patient's tenacity, persistence, or commitment is one trait that may separate those who gain from the rest.

We wondered why some patients have years of therapy with little change and then suddenly make rapid progress. We employed the term *readiness* to describe this state of a patient that seems to facilitate change. Then we tried to define it operationally. The *capacity to acknowledge distress* seemed to capture one aspect of it. Sufficient *motivation* to work hard was another factor. The *willingness to assume responsibility* for one's own behavior was the critical third feature.

Some patients orient themselves to the task of therapy by describing events in great detail, as well as the contribution and reaction of others to these events. They leave themselves out, accepting the role of observer instead of participant. It is possible, but unusual, to be able to change the behavior of another. With diligent effort, we seem to be able to make changes in ourselves. I recall a patient whom I had treated weekly for one year. She focused on "all the awful men who had mistreated her." One day, she decided to concentrate instead on herself (her beliefs and expectations of these men). We terminated successfully three months later.

Another factor that may contribute to readiness for change is the willingness to take prudent risks in the client's best interest (a parody of an old Dreyfus and Company commercial!). Most striking in the chronically depressed, but encountered in acute depression as well, is the lack of *willingness to risk*. Compounding the problem is a risk-assessment approach that sees risk in places where others seem virtually certain of a positive outcome.

The patient's view of the therapist and their relationship incorporates several factors that seem to affect change. A positive view (the therapist is seen as confident, involved, likable) is felt to facilitate the therapeutic work. There is a similar effect when the relationship is felt to be warm, safe, and stimulating of the patient's thinking. Although perhaps obvious, it seems that nothing succeeds quite like success. The patient's awareness that he or she is making progress appears to facilitate further progress.

A summary of the ten active ingredient patient factors is found in Table 2.

TABLE 2: PATIENT VARIABLES

1. Seeking help
2. Hope
3. Trust
4. Shared belief in therapist's method
5. Commitment (persistence)
6. Readiness
7. Sees therapist as confident, involved, likable
8. Sees relationship as warm, safe, stimulating
9. Experiences a sense of progress
10. Talks about him or herself, rather than circumstances or others

THE MATCH BETWEEN PATIENT AND THERAPIST

While there seem to be "good" patients and "good" therapists, who are each more skilled than some of their peers, "goodness of fit" may be another active ingredient in change. Early in my training, I was taught (by Marc Hollender, at the University of Pennsylvania) that a simple 2 × 2 table must be part of every patient evaluation (see Table 3).

In box 1, the focus is on the personality styles of the therapist and the patient. The implication is that similarities in dealing with data and relating to others facilitate a good working relationship. In box 2, the therapist's knowledge and familiarity with the patient's diagnosis and/or problem is spotlighted. I rarely treat schizophrenics, adolescents, or drug abusers. Most often, my patients are acutely or chronically depressed or anxious. Another group I work with has a rigidity of character style that impedes success or happiness. I try to refer the unmatched group to colleagues and to encourage referrals of the "good matches" to me.

Box 3 asks about the patient's expectations of the treatment. With dissemination of therapy–relevant information more widespread today, many patients choose a therapist at least in part for his or her model or approach. This box asks that the technique be one the patient believes is suitable for him or her. In the fourth box, the therapist is asked, "Is this technique likely to be useful for the patient's problem?" The attempt is made to challenge the notion that one approach works for everyone and to encourage the therapist to identify a match between technique and problem.

TABLE 3: THE MATCH BETWEEN PATIENT
AND THERAPIST

	PATIENT	PROBLEM
THERAPIST	1	2
TECHNIQUE	3	4

Given the strange (and occasionally wonderful) ways in which patient and therapist find each other, the notion of a match may strike some clinicians as arbitrary and unnecessary. Although there are additional active ingredient factors, I have found the match to be an important evaluation consideration. I have learned to refer those with whom I don't fit well to my colleagues.

PROCESS VARIABLES

This set of factors raises the question, "Does anything the therapist *does* make a difference or is the relationship the active factor in change?" I believe that the process contributes significantly to change. I also believe that some psychotherapies "package" the process factors more powerfully than others.

An early issue for the therapist to consider involves the patient's concept of what he or she must do in therapy. We believe that a clear understanding by the patient of his role facilitates change. Some patients referred for treatment have had substantial experience in psychotherapy. Some have read about it or heard about it from family or friends. Some still make the analogy to a doctor visit and expect to be the passive recipient of advice leading to relief. It has been shown that formal *role induction* instruction[2] helps to bring the less experienced patient up to speed.

Whatever the model of psychotherapy chosen, the patient is usually asked to become an observer of his or her own thoughts, feelings, and actions. No one model provided to explain the patient's distress has proven to be globally better than any competing model. More important, it seems, is to provide for the patient an explanation for his or her distress. It is of interest that the *provision of a myth* seems more important than its content.

I have found it useful to inquire about my patient's concept of anatomy, physiology, and even "how the mind works" (where relevant). Often these ideas have proven factually false. Some relief and relearning can be provided with simple, direct, corrective information.

For some (for example, depressed) persons, certain functions (expressivity, assertion, independence) are lacking because the necessary skills to perform them are lacking as well. These individuals need to be taught (by modeling, reading a book, suggestion and practice) how to add a lacking skill to their repertoire.

Three technique–based interventions that are a part of most psychotherapies are modeling, exposure, and mastery. Behavior therapists have described each of these most clearly. Watching the therapist engage in a behavior or approach a problem may overcome some patients' resistance to risk. For fears and phobias, actually confronting the feared object or situation may be a central ingredient in change. For the depressed, the experience of mastering a task or assignment in therapy may begin to challenge their belief in their own ineffectiveness.

For us, *reframing* as a process seemed to capture the essence of what therapists and patients *do* in addition to what they *are* for each other. Reframing is defined as: changing the conceptual and/ or the emotional setting or viewpoint with which something is held, seen, or understood. Placing the interpretation of an event or relationship in another framework may change its consequences and its meaning for the individual.

The cognitive therapist often calls this "breaking the set," for example, the negative cognitive set that dominates thinking in depression. Watzlawick, Weakland and Fisch[3] note how Tom Sawyer reframed the drudgery of whitewashing a fence into a pleasure for which participants had to pay. They discuss first–order change as a process of rearranging variables in the same field into different sequences. All factors remain within the original system. (My grandmother would compare this concept to housecleaning as a process of "moving the dust from one place to another.") In second–order change, however, there is a shift in the premises (rules) on which the system is based. This is the essence of reframing.

The nine–dot problem will be familiar to some readers (see Figure 1). The problem is insoluble given the assumption that all lines must originate and terminate within a mythical rectangle drawn around the dots. Once you challenge this assumption (free yourself from this limitation), many solutions present themselves (for one solution, see Figure 2). Focusing on the assumptions about the dots, rather than on the dots themselves, leads to the solution. This notion of reframing may be the process the patient describes

FIGURE 1: THE NINE-DOT PROBLEM

Connect the dots by four straight lines *without* lifting pencil from paper. (Taken from Watzlawick, Weakland, & Fisch, 1974.)

FIGURE 2: THE NINE-DOT PROBLEM SOLUTION

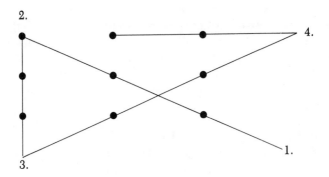

First-order change: One attempts to solve the task within the ("assumed") rectangle.

Second-order change: Examine not the dots, but the assumptions about the dots.

(Taken from Watzlawick, Weakland, & Fisch, 1974.)

TABLE 4: PROCESS VARIABLES

1. Role induction
2. Patient becomes an observer
3. Providing an explanatory system
4. Providing corrective information
5. Teaching new skills
6. Facilitating perspective
7. Modeling
8. Exposure
9. Mastery
10. Reframing

when he says: "I still have some of the same problems I had when I began therapy, but I feel (think) differently about them."

The process factors are summarized in Table 4.

$\mathrm{P}\overline{\quad}^2$ractical
Psychotherapy

I have been fortunate to be invited to many lecture halls to speak about cognitive therapy over the past 18 years. Several of my hosts have taken the liberty of suggesting titles for my presentation. Their suggestions (most of which I have taken) illustrate the understanding they have (with variable exposure to the system) of the cognitive model for psychotherapy.

I was invited to Memphis to lecture by Hagop Akiskal, professor of psychiatry at the University of Tennessee. Finding traditional psychotherapy ideas to be too often muddled, he asked me to speak about "Practical Psychotherapy for Depression." Barney Carroll, soon after becoming chairman of psychiatry at Duke, asked me to speak about "Psychotherapy in the Real World." His concern was that some academicians had lost touch with the systems guiding some private practitioners in their outpatient work. In Buffalo, Murray Morphy adapted a version of the old campaign slogan of Adlai Stevenson, coming up with "Cognitive Therapy: Talking Sense to the American Patient." He expressed the worry that psychotherapy was too often jargon–filled for his taste.

Psychotherapy is a process for educating (or sometimes reeducating) the patient. Bearing in mind that most patients present for therapy because of distress, and not to educate themselves, psychotherapists must offer the hope of relief from distress. If not cure, which I believe is a rare outcome, psychotherapy must "help" the patient. The patient seeks change.

This acknowledged, there are certain practical considerations that I believe are necessary for any psychotherapeutic system to work. Systematization of these ideas was stimulated by Dr. Akiskal's suggested title for my talk.

PRINCIPLES OF PRACTICAL PSYCHOTHERAPY

1. Educate the Patient About His or Her Clinical Condition

Patients have brought to my office a wide range of approaches to understanding the nature of their distress, from the curse of the Devil or the will of God to chemical derangement, hereditary taint, parental models, lack of necessary skills, laziness and ineptitude, and more. One task of the psychotherapist is to present a clear understanding of the psychopathology to the patient. This may serve to challenge and counteract the patient's attempt to attribute his or her distress to an external, irreversible source.

2. Educate and Engage Significant Others

Traditional psychotherapy has taught that interaction with someone other than the identified patient may dilute the effectiveness of the treatment. Family systems approaches have argued that the *patient* is only the system's way of *defining* the problem. Since the "distress" is in the system, several persons may have to be involved in the therapy to achieve change.

I have taken a middle route. I don't believe it is necessary to see everyone in the patient's family in every case. However, significant information is often forthcoming from someone other than the patient. I encourage gaining access to this information by meeting with a significant other, either accompanied by or in the absence of the patient him or herself. The configuration is often dictated by the level of trust within the family system. The need to maintain the patient's confidentiality may make this meeting a difficult, one-way transaction, but for me it has nearly always been worthwhile. Family members frequently have questions about anxiety or depressive syndromes that can be answered in a straightforward fashion. Commonly, they want to know how they can best help. Sometimes they reveal their own distress or shed light on how they may contribute to the patient's problem. In this instance, a referral for help can lead to major familial gain.

3. Maintain Your Optimism and Mobilize the Patient's Hope

I have often been asked, "Since you seem like such an 'up' person, how do you do it, seeing so many depressed people and listening to their problems all day?" My optimism is rooted in the belief that depressive and anxiety disorders are two of the most responsive conditions to treatment. At some point, I usually tell my patients that I have seen many like themselves change markedly in a short time.

Mobilizing hope, particularly in someone who is depressed and hopeless, seems like a contradictory expectation. The contradiction is resolved if you consider hope in a narrow, defined sense. It is possible, I have found, for a depressed person to maintain simultaneously a pessimistic outlook on the future and an attitude of hope about the likelihood of the therapy to achieve a desired result.

4. Identify and Utilize the Patient's Resources

At the risk of reducing to the concrete some of the abstract aspects of change in psychotherapy, I have often presented their task to my patients as "using the practical, goal-directed approach you have applied in the past to such tasks as fixing your car to the problem of fixing your thinking." Certainly, some people are clinically depressed or anxious because they lack a skill that would enable them to be more effective. In these cases, that skill may be *taught* to them in the therapy. In many cases, however, the necessary skills are already present, but the patient is "obstacled" from utilizing them. Identification and removal of these obstacles enable the patient to put his or her usual resources to work on the problem. This may be, for some, the definition of the cognitive work of therapy: removing the obstacle.

5. Teach Skills When They Are Lacking

My mother told me many years ago that she strongly preferred that I never become a teacher (like her). I guess I both followed and abandoned her advice. Cognitive therapy has been fairly called a "psychoeducational treatment." At its most specific, it may identify a skill that is lacking and devise a way to teach that skill to the patient. Some skills that come to mind are assertiveness, expression of feelings, and decision-making. Methods to convey those skills include modeling by the therapist, assignment of relevant readings, and the generation of appropriate alternatives in a specified situation.

6. Accept the Patient

Early in my career, I injudiciously told a bright and prolific supervisee that I felt that I could help any patient whom I "liked." While I have learned from experience that the statement is naive (and that I might at least have specified "any *motivated* patient"), I believe this quality of acceptance is central to a successful therapeutic outcome. Experience has taught me that I can find "something to like" in many patients. When first impressions are negative, I sometimes "grow to like" a patient over time. When I believe a patient and I are a "bad match," I make an effort to refer him or her to someone more suitable.

7. Encourage the Patient to Become Self-Observant

Beck and his colleagues[4] have written about the patient's adopting the orientation of viewing himself as the object of scientific inquiry. In point of fact, the patient in cognitive therapy is encouraged to identify relevant thoughts and to analyze them by noting errors in thinking. This capacity of "taking distance from oneself" and viewing thoughts, feelings, and behavior more objectively may be a central feature of all psychotherapy.

8. Provide Structure When Needed

Particularly for the acutely anxious or acutely depressed person, the defining of limits or the establishment of an approach to a problem may, by itself, bring some relief. Often the capacity to establish and utilize structure is lost early in a crisis situation. The methods of successive approximation or modeling may help the patient regain a lost sense of mastery and lead to the discovery of solutions to problems.

9. Discourage Major Decision-Making

It is a tenet of traditional psychotherapy that the period of treatment is often ill-suited to the making of major decisions. The cognitive model suggests that thinking in acute emotional states may be distorted and, therefore, unrepresentative of the patient's usual cognitive output. It stands to reason that, under these conditions, decisions reached may not reflect the patient's "usual" values, priorities, or choices. Therefore, it is recommended that major decisions (e.g., leaving a job or spouse) might better be postponed until the distortions are no longer dominant.

10. Encourage Appropriate Risk-Taking

Particularly among the depressed and the chronically passive, there is often a reluctance to take risks. The probability assessment that ordinarily precedes risking may be wildly distorted. Ask, for example, a person phobic of flight travel what the probability is of his or her plane crashing. Ask the socially anxious man or woman what the probability is of being turned down when he or she asks someone out on a date. Ask the anxious parent what the probability is of his or her child's accepting advice or a limit. Ask the timid employee what the probability is of the boss granting his or her request for a raise. Often I have found it helpful to identify with the patient some serious, some "middling," and some minor risks. Then the clinician can discuss the restrictions imposed by the refusal to risk and the benefits that may result from taking reasonable risks.

11. Provide the Patient With an Explanatory System

Although Frank[1] has maintained that the content of the explanation is secondary to its provision, I believe it is critical for the system to be one that the patient can comprehend. I have found that the notion of cognitions driving affects and behaviors is a simple one for most patients to grasp. The mastery that often results from viewing thoughts objectively, defining errors consistently made, and trying out alternatives forms for me a solid endorsement of the cognitive model.

12. Encourage the Generation of Alternative Beliefs

All psychotherapies do this. Cognitive therapy perhaps approaches it most directly. Critical beliefs are identified; consistent errors in thinking are pointed out; then new options or alternate choices are found, and their consequences are examined. Experiments may be done to test the new choices.

13. Encourage (Provide) Mastery Experiences

Again, successful psychotherapy will either present or lead to opportunities for mastery. Cognitive therapy does this directly in the psychotherapeutic work. When an individual no longer feels himself a "prisoner" of his or her distorted thinking, a sense of mastery over one's thoughts may lead to powerful changes in feelings and behavior.

14. Facilitate the Regaining of Perspective

This is the central principle of crisis intervention treatment. In most short-term psychotherapy, the regaining of lost perspective is one way of looking at a successful outcome. Once more, cognitive therapy approaches this practical need concretely. This may take the form of a shift of priorities, the acceptance of a limit, or the acknowledgment that "outcomes" cannot be controlled.

WHAT DOES A COGNITIVE THERAPIST TREAT?

Cognitive therapy began as a model for the treatment of acute depression.[4] A logical application to acute anxiety disorders followed.[5] What began as individual psychotherapy has been applied in work with groups,[6] and what began as a short-term model has been extended for long–term, character problems (see Chapter 9).

When I mentioned at a lecture that schizophrenia is not usefully approached with this model, I was handed a doctoral dissertation challenging this notion (see, for example, *Cognitive Therapy With Schizophrenic Patients*[7]). I believe that the borderline patient is often beyond the reach of cognitive therapy; however, others (e.g., John Rush at Southwestern Medical School in Dallas) routinely employ the language of cognitive therapy in these cases.

Although all of my work has been with outpatients, cognitive therapy is used with inpatients[8]; in fact, many psychiatric hospitals have established inpatient units that employ the cognitive model.

Although I have worked exclusively with adults, there are reports of successful outcomes with children.[8] There are reports of successful cognitive interventions to treat phobic patients, substance abusers, and those with sexual dysfunctions.[8] Beck[9] has recently written about using a cognitive approach to explore relationship problems among couples.

WHO IS A CANDIDATE?

Clinicians frequently hope that an alternative model will provide a framework to approach those patients they find most difficult to treat. While cognitive therapy has been applied in some of these cases (particularly when the patient has derived little benefit from psychoanalytic treatment), in the main a good candidate for traditional therapy will be a good candidate for cognitive therapy as well. The capacity to be introspective (or psychologically minded) is one requisite. If the patient can't identify automatic thoughts or can't work on a conceptual level, this approach will usually not be fruitful. The patient expecting magical answers or demanding that the therapist do the work will usually not succeed with this model.

It is clear to me that age, in and of itself, predicts neither success nor failure in psychotherapy. The patient who fails to engage does no better in cognitive therapy than elsewhere. Those unmotivated to change offer the same challenge to the cognitive therapist as to more traditional clinicians. I know of no answer for them.

THE COURSE OF THERAPY

It seems to take about three to five sessions to teach a motivated patient the cognitive model. For a few, this will suffice as treatment, since the structure of the method will support hope and a sense of mastery. Using the techniques may combat demoralization and help these patients regain perspective. Their own resources will then take over to help them deal with the problems they face. For them, therapeutic contact ends at this point. They may call or return at a later date.

For most patients, short–term cognitive therapy is prescribed to deal with acute depression or anxiety. Therapy may last from three to six months, involving 10–20 (usually weekly) sessions. Antidepressant medication may accompany treatment in appropriate depressed patients.

For character (personality) problems, long–term cognitive therapy may require several years of work. The frequency of contact remains once weekly. A focus on schemas replaces that on cognitions in the short–term model. Relationship elements receive special consideration (see Chapter 9).

For both short and long–term courses, follow-up visits at increasing intervals (usually beginning at one month and preceding to three to six months) may be scheduled subsequent to termination (see Chapter 12).

TRAINING IMPLICATIONS

It is the job of the good teacher to engage his or her students. I have found this to be most challenging in those settings in which psychodynamics are taught as basic to *all* psychotherapy. This problem is compounded by a course placement late in the student's training. My first opportunity to teach cognitive therapy at Georgetown was with fourth–year psychiatric residents. Subsequently, second–year residents were presented with the model at a time before their views of intervention choice had hardened. This was more enjoyable (for both teacher and students) and more successful.

One engagement technique is to demonstrate the method by

having the students apply it to a problem in living of their own. Once they demonstrate the capacity to frame a personal situation in cognitive language, the application to patient issues is facilitated.

A frequently encountered problem for me as a teacher has been the opposition provided by some psychoanalytically oriented supervisors. Since the supervisory group often wields considerable influence with the trainees, engaging this group may be a prerequisite for a successful learning experience with the students.

There is little that can aid the trainee in visualizing the technique of therapy like viewing the teacher behind a one-way mirror or on videotape. An opportunity to ask questions or generate alternative approaches following the demonstration complements this approach.

The up-to-date clinical program, whether in psychiatry, social work or psychology, should present the model early, provide role models of cognitive therapists as teachers and supervisors, require that some patients be treated and reviewed, assign representative readings, and convey an acceptance of the cognitive model as "one of the roads to Rome."

II

The
Cognitive Model

3

Prelude to the
Cognitive Model

Psychotherapy is traditionally considered to be a long-term venture. Meaningful changes made by patients are thought to involve character structure (or personality). The therapist, in psychodynamic psychotherapy, serves as a passive guide for the patient, who seeks illumination of the present in understanding events of the past. A prominent role is assigned to the unconscious. In this place, to which access is available via dreams, free associations and inferences, reside the thoughts and feelings that conflict with the realities facing the distressed individual.

The relationship of patient to therapist, if kept sufficiently free of realistic details, is thought to serve as a mirror into the determinants of significant relationships in the past, as well as a reflection of the formulations governing relationships in general. This has been called transference. Its counterpart in the therapist (thoughts and feelings about the patient that divert his or her attention from the task at hand) has been called countertransference.

The testing of assumptions and the "working through" of feelings about the therapeutic relationship are seen by many psychodynamic therapists as an important road to change for the patient. These characteristics associated with psychodynamic psychotherapy are summarized in Table 5.

BRIEF THERAPY

The assumption that therapy must be long-term has been challenged effectively by Budman[10] and others. In brief therapy, the therapist and patient agree to a contract specifying termination after about three to six months (10 to 20 sessions). This is a "prospective judgment" made during the evaluation phase of psycho-

TABLE 5: AN OVERVIEW OF CHARACTERISTICS OF
PSYCHODYNAMIC PSYCHOTHERAPY

---

1. Long-term
2. Oriented to character change
3. Often dwells in the past
4. Often prescribes a passive role for the therapist
5. Assigns a prominent role to the unconscious
6. Emphasizes the therapist-patient relationship (so-called "transference")

---

therapy (not a retrospective judgment made after therapy ends prematurely!).

Some have suggested that one factor determining the lengthiness of psychotherapy is "psychotherapeutic perfectionism."[10] Psychotherapy, the argument goes, aims at "cure" or "complete change" and anything short of this is unacceptable. The counterargument asks of therapy that it "be helpful," that it facilitate relief from distress. Consumer demand and third–party payment, prominent influences in the 1970s and '80s, have supported more focal and less lengthy psychotherapies.

With this shift in emphasis has come a move away from the psychodynamic perspective on growth and development (psychosexual stages, regressions, and fixations) and movement toward a life-cycle (Eriksonian) concept of development.[11] In this approach, critical periods of development are identified throughout the life cycle in which "ego qualities" emerge. These "eight ages of man" begin with basic trust and proceed through autonomy, initiative, industry, identity, intimacy, generativity, and ego integrity. This approach leads to treatment that is periodic (rather than continuous), emphasizes follow-up (even when well), and offers the therapist's tong-term availability for future consultation.

What does this brief therapy look like? Most often, it is time-limited. Goals are discussed and agreed upon by therapist and patient during the evaluation. The focus is maintained in the here-and-now, with only occasional brief forays into the past for some specific purpose. The therapist's role is "active," with the interaction more often a dialogue than a patient monologue. A premium is placed upon rapid assessment, therapeutic flexibility, and careful patient selection. The characteristics of brief therapy are summarized in Table 6.

Cognitive therapy is but one model among several that qualify as brief therapy. Behavior therapy was a predecessor, now firmly established as a useful approach to habit change. The work of Joseph Wolpe[12] in the late 1950s is generally credited with stimulating clinicians to apply the principles of learning theory to help clients change behavior. Applying laboratory findings from studies of lower animals to their human analogues led to the formulation of techniques and strategies for treating clinical anxiety, depression, sexual problems, and substance abuse. In addition, "habits" like cigarette smoking, stuttering, and overeating have been approached by behavioral analysis and intervention.

Systematic desensitization, a technique derived from classical conditioning that combines deep muscle relaxation with graded exposure to an anxiety–evoking stimulus, was an early suggestion for treating anxiety disorders. The token economy system, derived from operant conditioning, was adopted as a structure for the inpatient treatment of some severe emotional disorders.

The brief behavior therapy approach stressed an initial behavioral analysis to identify antecedent and consequent conditions of

TABLE 6: CHARACTERISTICS OF BRIEF THERAPY

1. Time-limited
2. Goal-oriented
3. Here-and-now focus
4. Active role for the therapist
5. Rapid assessment
6. Therapeutic flexibility
7. Opportunity to ventilate
8. Rapid formation of a therapeutic alliance
9. Careful patient selection

Derived from Budman, S. (1985). *Forms of brief therapy*. New York: Guilford.

the behavior to be changed. Then a baseline measure was made of the behavior before therapy began. Finally, a paradigm or strategy derived from learning theory was designed as a basis for intervention. Careful measurements were made to document change when it occurred. Booster sessions were available should problems recur.

Social skills that were lacking were taught by didactic presentation, reading assignments, modeling, coaching and roleplaying. Written materials were employed to chart activity, monitor mood, track changes, and provide reinforcement for change.

Behavior therapy principles emphasized structure, applied theories of reinforcement, encouraged self-monitoring, and focused on goal attainment. Adherents initially stressed the necessity for all variables considered to be observable. By definition, this requirement excluded cognition. Over the past decade there has been a convergence of cognitive and behavior therapists, as a willingness has developed to consider thoughts as "acceptable data" for psychotherapy.

Interpersonal psychotherapy (ITP) was developed by Gerald Klerman and Myrna Weissman[13] in the late 1970s. It aims to provide a short-term interventive focus for problems related specifically to grieving, the resolution of role disputes, role transitions, and interpersonal deficits. Initially designed for the depressed patient, this system emphasizes the relationship of disruption or deprivation of attachment bonds to the onset of depression. Through a renegotiation of the interpersonal circumstances relevant to the individual's emotional state, practitioners seek to reduce depressive symptoms and improve functioning. There is liberal use made here of both cognitive and behavioral principles and techniques. Sessions are once weekly, and therapy is planned to last for three to four months.

Approaches to the identified interpersonal problems include outlining the issues, expectations, wants, options, and resources of the patient and his or her spouse. Parallels with previous relationships may be drawn. The "interpersonal strategy" of each individual may be discussed and contrasted. Finally, alternative approaches and their consequences are considered.

In response to the stress on shorter and more focal psychotherapy in the '70s and '80s, the psychodynamic schools developed delivery systems to compete with the brief therapies. Peter Sifneos,[14] James Mann,[15] David Malan,[16] and Habib Davanloo[17] are among the major contributors in this regard.

COGNITIVE THERAPY

Cognitive therapy was formulated in the early 1960s by Aaron Beck at the University of Pennsylvania. Contributions were made by Michael Mahoney[18] and Donald Meichenbaum.[19] There are many similarities and overlaps between this work and the Rational-Emotive Therapy (RET) approach of Albert Ellis.[20] Furthermore, students of each of the above have written and extended the model and its usefulness.

A comprehensive review of the many streams of cognitive therapy is available elsewhere[21]; here I will concentrate instead on presenting the system as it was taught to me by Beck in 1969–71 and as I have employed it in my practice of psychotherapy.

As a model for psychotherapeutic intervention, cognitive therapy[22] seeks to:

1. Identify cognitions relevant to the presenting problem
2. Recognize connections among cognitions, affects, and behaviors
3. Examine the evidence for and against key beliefs
4. Encourage the patient to try out alternative conceptualizations
5. Teach the patient to carry out the cognitive process independently

Beck[22] elaborated specific changes in the form and content of thinking for a broad range of clinical problems. He then applied the model to clinical depression, hypomania, anxiety, phobia, paranoid state, hysteria, obsessions, and compulsions. Since the earliest applications concentrated upon clinical depression,[23,24,25] let us follow the elaboration of the model with depression as an example.

A COGNITIVE MODEL
OF DEPRESSION

It is said that a depressed person's thinking more closely resembles that of another depressed person than it does his or her own thinking prior to the onset of the depression. In form, conceptualization becomes more *global*, universal, and all-encompassing. There is a dominance of "shoulds" that has been called *moralistic*. In content, the depressed individual usually sees the disorder as an *irreversible* change. As the depression extends and deepens, he or she views the world more and more narrowly, constricting his or her focus to *personalistic* concerns. A tendency, sometimes present in the premorbid state and sometimes new to the depressed condition, is to think in a *dichotomous* fashion. People, events, and situations are seen as black or white (polarized). There is no middle ground — no grays, no alternatives to the categorical extremes. Some qualities of thinking in depression are noted in Table 7.

As a depression develops, predictable distortions occur in the patient's thinking.[25] A hypothetical look at the evolution of depression in an individual will illustrate one application of the cognitive model to help understand a clinical problem. Two predisposing factors mark the starting point of development. The first is early loss (for example, of a parent who dies or leaves) or rejection. The second is the learning of perfectionistic standards that limit later adaptability.

Two kinds of precipitating events may mark the onset of the depressive disorder. The first is some significant subtraction from

TABLE 7: QUALITIES OF
DEPRESSIVE THINKING

1. Global
2. Moralistic
3. Irreversible
4. Personalistic
5. Dichotomous

Derived from Beck, A. T. (1967). *Depression: Clinical, experimental and theoretical aspects.* New York: Harper & Row.

the patient's personal domain (the sum total of traits, values, and issues considered important by the patient). The second is a chronic gap between the patient's expectations and outcomes.

Initially, the meaning assigned to the precipitating event is *polarized* by the depressed person. The patient's focus narrows to the negative aspects of the event, to the exclusion of the positives. Finally, the focus shifts to (and gets stuck on) the self. The depressed person "jumps to negative conclusions" about him or herself. These have been called *arbitrary inferences* or conclusions derived from insufficient data. Selecting one detail out of context and magnifying its significance is a second common cognitive error; this has been called *selective abstraction*. The self-view of the patient is modified to see him or herself as deficient or defective.

Now depressive schemas dominate the patient's thinking. A schema is a unit of belief, a principle or main organizing idea. Schemas are formed early in life through the influence of role models, direct feedback, cultural factors, and early experience. When depressed, these negative schemas (like large "pipes") hypertrophy, so that much of the data input is filtered through them. The result is a broad range of *negative generalizations* about the self. These generalizations support a growing tendency to personalize events and situations, to become extremely self-critical and self-blaming. They are soon extended to encompass input about the world and the future as well as the self.

This globally negative cognitive set (negative orientation of the patient's thinking) leads to behavioral *withdrawal*. Apathy and *loss of motivation* follow. Physical symptoms of depression appear: disrupted sleep, appetite loss, constipation, low energy, easy fatigue, poor concentration, and diminished attention span. A *feedback loop* in which the patient's appraisal of his or her own negativity creates more negativity, now worsens the condition. Low self-worth, pessimism, and helplessness are common cognitive consequences. Suicidal ideas may be organized around a theme of escape, cessation (relief), or punishment.

Withdrawal is often complemented by *passivity* (unwillingness to risk; little behavioral initiative) and an increase in escape and avoidance behaviors. Now, the patient's usual activities and obligations cannot be undertaken. He or she is often out of work, functioning poorly in relationships, and extremely dissatisfied with him or herself. The downward slide into depression is summarized in Table 8.

Understanding clinical problems like depression within the framework of a cognitive model prepares the therapist–patient team to attack the problem with cognitive therapy. The model will be explained in detail in Chapter 4. A broad range of therapeutic techniques will follow in Chapter 5.

TABLE 8: DEVELOPMENT OF A DEPRESSION

1. Polarization of key event
2. Selective focus on the negative
3. Focus stuck on the self
4. Negative generalizations about the self
5. Negative generalizations about the world and the future
6. Behavioral withdrawal
7. Loss of motivation
8. Physical symptoms of depression appear
9. Feedback loop worsens syndrome
10. Passivity and escape and avoidance behaviors increase

Derived from Beck, A.T. (1967). *Depression: Clinical, experimental, and theoretical aspects.* New York: Harper & Row.

4

Cognitive Model: The Basics

It is my hope that the readership of this book includes clinicians of differing backgrounds in training and some students who are not committed yet to psychology, medicine, or social work. If this hope is borne out, these opening words will have relevance only to those committed to some other system (e.g., psychoanalytic, behavioral) but not to the truly open-minded (whether they're eclectic clinicians or students not yet paying their dues to one system of psychotherapy).

If you have joined a particular school of thought, I ask you now to attempt to lay aside its basic assumptions (for a while). If you don't, you face the danger of trying to learn the cognitive model within the language you already use. For this reason, a paradigm shift is in order for those already committed to a system other than the cognitive one.

Attempting such a paradigm shift raises questions of motivation, flexibility, and security. Motivationally, why do you need to consider an alternative way of understanding people and problems? Is there something in it for you? For your patients or clients? For the clinician seeking to add some techniques to his or her armamentarium, I believe that the interventions are of little value alone, without their theoretical underpinning.

Particularly for those of us who have been doing therapy for quite a while, it is difficult to retain the flexibility that permits looking at a problem in a different way. There is a tendency to say that the alternative represents nothing new or to translate it into more familiar concepts. Finally, many of us seem to require the "membership" that accompanies belonging to a particular "union," whether it be behavioral, analytic, or biological. Over time, we make this a part of our identity, so that suspending it, even for a brief time, may be an overwhelming challenge.

Now that we have set aside restricting assumptions, let us proceed with the four components of the cognitive model: basic principles, the automatic thought, cognitive errors, and cognitive schemas. I will discuss each in turn.

BASIC PRINCIPLES

The cognitive therapist understands the person as an information–processing organism, one who takes in data (from both outside sources and inside readings) and generates appraisals. The individual's feelings and behavior are seen to be influenced in the here-and-now by one's thoughts. Most patients come to my office wishing to change some element of how they feel or what they do. If one of the therapeutic pair doubts that thoughts, feelings, and actions are related, it is likely that changing the latter two by working with the former won't make much sense. Here is one point at which a "shared belief in the therapist's method" truly comes into play!

The cognitive therapist believes that humans are capable of altering their thinking by dealing with conscious processes. A question commonly asked by psychoanalytically oriented colleagues is, "Do you believe in an unconscious?" In fact, I believe that the concept is a useful one, but it plays no role in the psychotherapy I do.

A second question, often posed from the analytic viewpoint, concerns the importance and therapeutic utility of exploring the past. The cognitive model does not dwell on the past. It is evident that cognitions (thoughts, assumptions, expectations) must have their origins prior to their emergence in the present. Indeed, some beliefs are seen to be learned quite early in life. However, one's cognitive set (the totality of an individual's beliefs, values, and appraisals) is constantly subject to modification. Surely, those beliefs held longest and given the most support will be the most difficult to dislodge. The original "learning" of these cognitions occurs by role-modeling, by feedback from significant figures, by the powerful effects of culture, and by experience. It seems logical that cognitive distortions (which form the basis for clinical problems) are learned the same way.

While the first set of principles of the cognitive model relates to our understanding the patient and his or her problems, the next group focuses on the process of psychotherapy itself. Therapy attempts to harness the patient's usual problem-solving skills. When certain skills are absent (e.g., assertiveness, expressivity, independence), these may be taught as part of the treatment.

Psychotherapy is an active, collaborative venture between therapist and patient. The story is told that an analytic failure is typically assigned to the patient, while a behavior therapy failure is typically seen as the responsibility of the therapist. In cognitive therapy, the collaborating pair takes the credit for success or the blame for failure.

Psychotherapy remains rooted in the here-and-now. Although an initial history may examine the origins of some key beliefs in the past, and some patients insist on tracing a relevant cognition back to its root, the active ingredients for change are seen to exist in the present. The therapist may reorient the patient to the present with comments such as, "Of course the idea came from somewhere. Our task now, however, is to determine what you want to do about it, and then to develop some alternatives."

One of the code words of the analytic method is "transference." For a while, the reverence with which it was treated in conversations among clinicians convinced me that it had some mystical meaning. I ventured one time to suggest to an analytic colleague that it meant that the sum of thoughts and feelings attached to a significant figure in the past forms the basis of appraising a person in the present. When he seemed nearly satisfied, I wondered why such a to-do was made over a concept that seemed so obvious.

Change in cognitive therapy is not understood in terms of transference. The therapeutic relationship may serve as a vehicle for examining beliefs and appraisals, but more often the subject is another relationship of the patient or the patient himself. The therapist is active and collaborative, hardly the traditional "blank screen." Self-disclosure, when done within limits (see Chapter 5), is not proscribed in this model. A summary statement might be that in cognitive therapy change can occur without dealing with transferential material directly.

THE CENTRAL CONCEPT OF THE
AUTOMATIC THOUGHT

For many of you, an understanding of the core concept in the cognitive model will involve a trip back to the teachings of college psychology. A basic learning principle was taught to me in terms of stimulus-response. This was illustrated (in my day) with the example of Pavlov's dog. The dog would salivate in response to the presentation of the stimulus of food. You could elicit the same response (salivation) to a different stimulus (e.g., a bell) if you paired the ringing of the bell (conditioned stimulus) with the presentation of the food (unconditioned stimulus). After a few trials, the dog would respond with salivation to the sound of the bell alone.

The stimulus-response learning paradigm we will focus on concerns *stimulus events or situations.* The responses are *feelings (reactions) or behaviors (actions).* For example, if you went to your boss this morning to ask for a raise and he or she said, "no," you might be angry. But you also might be sad, relieved, or anxious. There are several likely responses to the same stimulus event. A clue to the response is available in the variable that occurs between stimulus and response — the intervening variable (see Figure 3).

FIGURE 3: THE AUTOMATIC THOUGHT

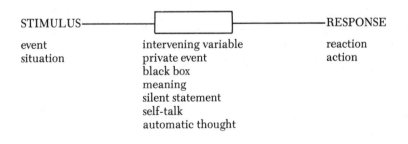

STIMULUS		RESPONSE
event	intervening variable	reaction
situation	private event	action
	black box	
	meaning	
	silent statement	
	self-talk	
	automatic thought	

Since this intervening variable is not directly observable, it has been called a "private event." It is elicited by asking the patient or client to examine his or her thinking and to supply it for the therapist. It has been referred to as the "silent statement people tell themselves."[26] Using this formulation, Meichenbaum explains how people describe, elaborate, or appraise a situation before they react to it. This intervening process between event and reaction has also been called "self-talk." In plainest English, this process supplies the *meaning* to the stimulus, guiding the selection of a response. Beck has defined the intervening variable as the *automatic thought*.[25]

My wife has occasionally awakened me in the middle of the night with the question, "Do you hear that noise downstairs?" Whether I do or do not is immaterial. Next she says, "Please go downstairs and see if there is someone in the house." My immediate response (usually unstated) is, "If there is someone in the house, what good would it do for me to go downstairs?" Protests rarely neutralize the urgency of the request. Most often, sleepy and skeptical, I comply and get out of bed. As I reach the top of the stairs and hear the noise, my palms are wet, my heartbeat is apparent to me and rapid, and my thoughts center around the themes of danger, unpreparedness, intrusion, and fear. Can you guess a few of my automatic thoughts?

I never quite know whether or not to turn on the light. If I am "surprising an intruder," this act would surely compromise the element of surprise. On the other hand, my general clumsiness at this hour and under these circumstances has undoubtedly already announced my impending arrival on the scene. So I turn on the light. At the bottom of the stairs, I hear the noise again. Looking out the front window. I can see the shutter being blown by the wind. When the shutter hits the siding of the house, the noise is produced. Very rapidly, I think, "It's harmless. There is no danger. I'm relieved." By the time I reach the top of the stairs, my heart rate has returned to normal, my hands are dry, and I am anxious to return to sleep. Armed with a different set of automatic thoughts, I return to bed, often annoyed at being awakened "for nothing." Note how the testing of my original assumptions facilitated their rapid replacement by a more rational set of beliefs.

Have you ever been in a country where the native language is one other than your own? Once, in that situation I walked past a group of eight young guys on a street corner and they instantly burst out laughing. I thought, "Must be doing something wrong here; something funny; look out of place." I felt anxious, uncomfortable. Most likely, it occurred to me later, someone among them had told a joke and they had all laughed. My behavior was probably not significant to anyone but myself.

This is an everyday experience and not just for travelers. For the hearing impaired, it is common to be unable to receive the usual auditory cues available to "anyone within earshot." Typically, the individual "fills in the blanks" as best he or she can. Sometimes the guesses are wrong, with embarrassment, humiliation, or occasionally, humor resulting. For one patient of mine, this led to social anxiety and avoidance of situations in which people would gather. He admitted sadly that he could not go to parties. The fundamental problem was not in the party, or in the real hearing impairment he suffered; rather, it was in the self-talk: the silent statements he was making to himself; his automatic thoughts. With diligent cognitive work aimed at identifying and challenging the relevant beliefs, this man was able to make a different adaptation to a social situation. It enabled him to attend, even to enjoy, a party for the first time in years. The change involved accepting his limitations and quieting his concern about the expected reactions of others to his request to "listen to something again."

In summary, the same stimulus can give rise to different responses depending upon the meanings assigned. In Rational-Emotive Therapy, a similar system is described in terms of ABC: the stimulus event (A), the automatic thought (B), and the response (C). At workshops, psychoanalytic colleagues often say that the automatic thoughts are familiar to them in their work with patients, then they suggest that they are unconscious. My standard response is that we can be made aware of this channel of self-talk merely by having our attention called to it — the accepted psychoanalytic definition of "preconscious," not unconscious.

Characteristics of automatic thoughts have been described by Beck.[22] Automatic thoughts are specific and discrete. They often occur not in full sentences but in a kind of shorthand, telegraphic form. Invariably, they are seen by the patient as plausible. Their content is idiosyncratic to the individual person having them, but there are similarities among patients with similar conditions (e.g., anxiety, depression, paranoia). They may provide clues, without invoking unconscious mechanisms, to unexpected reactions in individuals. And so, one way to understand such phenomena as "success depressions," depression after childbirth, or emotional reactions to moving can be to investigate the relevant automatic thoughts.

This might be a good time to pause and recall a situation you have recently been in that has evoked a powerful reaction, feeling, or behavior. Try to identify the automatic thoughts associated with your reaction. If this is difficult, and you are a good "imager," conjure up an image of the situation. This sometimes brings back the associated silent statements in people to whom automatic thoughts do not come easily. Alternatively, recall an issue being discussed in your office by a patient. Try to infer the automatic thoughts of your patient from the presentation. Cognitive therapy does not have a monopoly on the appearance of, or work with, automatic thoughts. It is likely that you can find a referent for this in your own work or in your own life.

In the frequent presentations that I do, often I begin with evident speaking anxiety. Usually this reaction disappears as soon as I get "engaged" in my talk and "connect" with my audience. On one highly memorable occasion, this didn't happen. I was invited to share a workshop on cognitive therapy in Savannah, Georgia with a good friend and colleague. He suggested that I speak for the first hour, and I readily agreed to lead off. I noticed the usual anticipatory butterflies as I was being introduced and the usual initial performance anxiety as I began to speak. ("Would they think that my talk was worthwhile? Would they form a positive impression of me?") I had planned to tell a joke as an "engager." I told my story, and there was utterly no response. ("Must have been Northern humor," I thought, but didn't say.)

My anxiety level leaped several notches higher. I could hear my voice shake, began to feed back to myself how anxious I felt, and noticed that, instead of getting better, the nervousness was getting worse. I knew that getting involved in my talk would help me turn the corner; however, having failed to do it in the way I had planned, I was at a loss for how to proceed. Meanwhile, I was proceeding with my presentation in a shaky and unsure tone. I decided next to interrupt the flow (such as it was!) by pausing for a long drink of water. As my mouth was uncommonly dry (a typical anxiety symptom), this seemed like a good idea.

I was aware of speaking on one channel, having automatic thoughts on a second, and recording them on a third. ("What will they think when I stop? Do they know how nervous I am? What if I can't continue? This isn't going according to plan. Never happened to me quite like this before.") When I resumed, I made an offhand comment and noted an affirming look from a young woman sitting in the front of the audience. I began to speak directly to her, ignoring for the moment the other ninety-nine or so participants. I guess I "got into" my talk, because before long the audience was nodding, laughing, and clearly attending to my words. The hour passed quickly, so that I was almost reluctant to give up the floor to my colleague. Rational responses had replaced the anxiety–evoking and anxiety–affirming automatic thoughts. ("They didn't like my joke, but they did get involved in my talk. They looked like a group interested in the topic and motivated to learn. My bout with anxiety was a small initial problem, eventually dealt with in the usual fashion, by engagement. The presentation, in the end, was little different from most others I have done.") Anyone who has done more than a little bit of public speaking has probably had a similar experience.

COGNITIVE ERRORS

The identification of automatic thoughts forms a large part of the initial work in cognitive therapy. Once known, they are worked with in a variety of ways. One way is to identify the consistent errors in thinking that lead to the production of cognitive distortions that lead to symptomatology. These errors can be found in the everyday thinking of healthy individuals, but in the emotional disorders, they dominate the cognitive set and are applied uncritically to most incoming data.

Commonly we see three major errors, and four more specific

distortions (see Table 9). *Polarization*, or dichotomous thinking, refers to assigning meanings in polar opposite categories. It is the first major error. Everything is understood as either black or white. There are no grays. If you don't fit on one extreme, you must belong in the only other category — its opposite. A grade of 95–100% is an "A"; anything below 95% is an "F." Your appearance is perfect — or terrible. There are no gradations, no middle ground. Thinking is categorical, not dimensional.

The second major error is *personalization*. The individual can only think in terms of him or herself. When this person looks at his "television screen of life," he sees only himself, taking up the entire screen. Ask him about a relationship between two people he knows and he will tell you how they each relate to him. It is difficult for him to remove himself from the situation and give you an impression of his observations.

Overgeneralization is the third major error: drawing conclusions beyond the substance of the data. When someone is criticized for a specific action and responds that he or she feels like a "failure," this is the error being made. When an individual performs below his or her level of expectations and assumes that he or she can never do better, this may be overgeneralization as well.

Specific errors in thinking include *selective abstraction*: focusing on one detail out of context. When an individual who receives

TABLE 9: COGNITIVE ERRORS

MAJOR:
    Polarization
    Personalization
    Overgeneralization

SPECIFIC:
    Selective abstraction
    Discounting
    Arbitrary inference
    Catastrophizing

Derived from Beck, A.T. (1976). *Cognitive therapy and the emotional disorders.* New York: International Universities Press.

an excellent performance appraisal with one area of suggested improvement makes this error, he conveys the criticism but ignores the overall evaluation. *Discounting* refers to an inability to accept praise. A common response to a compliment is, "Anyone could have done it," or, "The accomplishment doesn't mean much, really." Making an *arbitrary inference* in common language is called "jumping to conclusions." Finally, *catastrophizing* (a term from RET) occurs when a person thinks in terms of the worst possible outcome.

COGNITIVE SCHEMAS

A schema is a relatively enduring unit of belief from which moment–to–moment cognitions are derived. These schemas are the *rules* that govern how an individual assigns meanings. Albert Ellis[20] has compiled a list of irrational beliefs that he believes occur with a high frequency in our population. Some of these common rules or schemas are presented in Table 10.

Given time and motivation, the basic rules that govern the thinking of each of us could be identified and described. These building blocks of a person's thinking are analogous to the framework of a house. The structure "in which you live" is laid on top of, and within this framework. In the analogy, that structure refers to the automatic thoughts that lend meaning to everyday life.

In the practice of short-term cognitive therapy, automatic thoughts form the basic data of treatment. The schemas from

TABLE 10: COMMON SCHEMAS, WITH PARTICULAR RELEVANCE TO DEPRESSION

1. In order to be happy, I must be successful.
2. In order to be happy, I must be accepted by all people, all the time.
3. In order to be happy, I must have a husband (wife).
4. My worth depends upon what others think of me.
5. I cannot work, therefore I am inadequate.
6. I've made a mistake, therefore I am inept.
7. If someone disagrees with me, he doesn't like me.

Derived from Ellis, A. (1962). *Reason and emotion in psychotherapy.* New York: Lyle Stuart.

which they derive may be evident or they may be elusive. Identifying these rules may not fall within the scope of a brief therapy. Even if identified. schemas are not often a subject of therapeutic work, due to the limitations of time and the goals set for change.

In long-term cognitive therapy, rather than aiming at achieving insight, resolving conflict, or making conscious the individual's unconscious wishes or fears, we attempt to identify these schemas and to make them the focus of the therapeutic work (see Chapter 9). As the central rules that guide an individual's thinking, the schemas are enduring and are anchored by a host of derived cognitions applied to daily experience. The work entailed in change, therefore, is lengthy and often tedious; it may require considerable perseverance by the therapist–patient team.

For example, the schema. "I require the approval of significant others before I can accept myself as adequate," is frequently held by chronically depressed individuals. The therapeutic task may be conceptualized as one of challenging the individual to develop an alternative rule to guide the determination of self–worth. This may entail a consideration of the models provided by significant others, multiple examples of feedback elicited by the patient in a wide range of situations over time, and his or her appraisal of performance. Guidelines for self–appraisal may have to be developed in those for whom seeking approval has obviated the necessity for self-evaluation.

THE MAJOR FEATURES OF COGNITIVE THERAPY

To highlight those aspects of the cognitive model that distinguish it from alternative ways of understanding a patient and a problem, let me now abstract these characteristics from the four components of the model. In addition, let us make the transition from a model of understanding to a structure for intervention.

On the basis of the theory, what does cognitive therapy look like? The transaction between therapist and patient is an *active, structured, collaborative dialogue*, as opposed to a passive patient monologue. The focus is set on the *here-and-now*, rather than concentrated upon the identification of origins in the past for problems in the present. Therapeutic talk is *goal-directed and problem-solving in orientation*, rather than aiming at achieving insight, resolving conflict, or making conscious the individual's unconscious wishes or fears.

Often the therapy is a *time-limited* venture, with weekly meetings and a planned number of sessions agreed to at the outset, rather than an open-ended, continuous exploration requiring more frequent sessions over a lengthy period of time. The assumption is made that *affect and behavior can be changed by gaining mastery over one's assumptions, beliefs, and appraisals*. *Homework* assignments usually complement the work done during the sessions, providing an opportunity to generate data, test automatic thoughts, or practice suggested alternatives. Interpretations of unconscious factors are *not* made. The so-called transference neurosis is *neither encouraged, assumed, nor interpreted as such*. These characteristics of cognitive therapy are summarized in Table 11.

TABLE 11: MAJOR FEATURES OF COGNITIVE THERAPY

1. An active, structured dialogue
2. Focus on the here-and-now
3. Goal-directed, problem-solving collaboration
4. Often time-limited
5. Assumes that affect and behavior are affected by how one thinks
6. Use of homework assignments
7. Interpretations of unconscious factors are not made
8. The "transference neurosis" is neither encouraged, assumed, nor interpreted as such

5
Techniques of
Cognitive Therapy

While director of continuing education in psychiatry at Georgetown, I once invited a highly esteemed psychoanalyst to speak about the "Treatment of the Adolescent Patient." He spent the better part of an hour roaming through psychoanalytic concepts of adolescence and anecdotes of patients he had treated. The audience appeared to be listening, but also seemed somewhat restless. Finally, one of my C.E. regulars interrupted the speaker with a question, "The title of your talk was the '*Treatment* of the Adolescent Patient.' When are you going to tell us something about *treatment*?" The speaker quickly lit and chainsmoked three cigarettes. When he replied, "That would be a whole other talk," I looked for the trapdoor that C.E. directors keep for occasions like these. This impression is indelibly marked on my brain and I try to honor its lesson whenever I speak to my colleagues: Clinicians often find models to be academically interesting; however, their prime investment is in learning something they can use with their patients.

Before turning to treatment techniques, let me address your (the reader's) expectations. It is generally accepted that behavior therapists, in discussing technique, have helped to define what many therapists (behavioral and nonbehavioral) do. So too, you will see, with cognitive therapy. Much of what is discussed in this chapter is, therefore, not likely to be brand-new. Many of you will have referents for these techniques in your practice; some of them are firmly grounded in common sense.

Perhaps some of the approaches that follow will capture for you the essence of the active ingredients of psychotherapeutic intervention, as discussed in Chapter 1. And, perhaps not. For me, cognitive therapy approaches what I believe to be the active process ingredients in their purest form.

An attempt has been made to categorize the interventions in a temporal way. Early in psychotherapy, the techniques that help to *provide structure and gain mastery* for the patient often dominate the treatment. Cognitive therapy progresses next toward interventions to help *break the set* (alter the determining viewpoints) of the patient with an emotional disorder. Finally, a patient, now open to new considerations, will begin to *generate alternatives* (novel ways to view situations and events relevant to the presenting problem).

TECHNIQUES TO PROVIDE
STRUCTURE AND GAIN MASTERY

This initial group of interventions borrows liberally from the behavior therapy arsenal. They are particularly useful for patients who are severely withdrawn and lack access to the introspective resources needed to do basic cognitive work. If vegetative signs of depression are prominent (e.g., sleep disorder, loss of appetite, weight loss, lack of energy, and extreme fatigue or lethargy), anti-depressant medication is often the first order of the day.

We still lack a clear delineation of symptoms in depression that respond differentially to drug therapy and psychotherapy. The suggestion even has been made[27] that acute depression as a syndrome clears similarly, whether treated with drugs or with psychotherapy. If this proves true, the rationale for psychotherapeutic treatment of depression may shift to the prevention of relapse and the attenuation of the course of this problem over time.

Response to drug therapy may return to the patient his or her capability to utilize the problem-solving approaches used prior to the onset of the illness. Then, a focus on the cognitive elements may usefully begin. For a patient with so-called endogenous depression for whom drug therapy is contraindicated for some reason, behavioral techniques may constitute the sole initial treatment. Additionally, behavioral approaches may be employed to engage the patient in the tasks of change and to demonstrate his or her capacity to be effective before cognitive therapy begins.

Record keeping is often an initial assignment. To provide a baseline measure of activity or thoughts, a daily log may be kept and reviewed at each session. For the severely withdrawn patient, structure may be developed by prescribing activities to be engaged in and then recorded in the log. Psychotherapy to aid in weight loss or smoking cessation often begins with records kept of caloric intake or the number of cigarettes smoked. In later stages, cognitions maintaining the habit will be identified and challenged. Records of automatic thoughts play a prominent role in later stages of therapy.

In taking a history, the cognitive therapist is oriented toward identifying problems that cluster around organizing themes. When difficulty is noted in different situations, identifying a common thread may permit *problem reduction*. Often, the automatic thoughts in situations as diverse as consulting with one's legal clients, talking on the phone with mother, and negotiating a decision with one's spouse may be reduced to a common pathway with similar cognitive elements (for example, a fear of confrontation). The patient may be shown early in psychotherapy that a change in his or her thinking, therefore, may bring widespread benefits.

In attaching meanings to events or situations, patients commonly mislabel or fail to label. *Accurate relabeling* may, by itself, provide significant relief. During my residency days at the University of Pennsylvania, I encountered a patient whose presentation illustrated a mislabeling problem. This 39–year–old man from a Middle Eastern country was a student at the business school. One month prior to coming to outpatient clinic, he experienced a series of episodes of chest pain and difficulty breathing. His father and a brother (each back home) had died of heart attacks at the age of 40. The patient went first to medical clinic, presenting himself as a man with coronary artery disease. A physical exam, electrocardiogram, and blood enzyme studies failed to support the diagnosis. He was referred to psychiatry and, upon arrival, assigned to me.

An alternative (and more accurate) explanation for his symptoms was that they were manifestations of an anxiety reaction. Since death is an infrequent outcome of anxiety, this relabeling brought some relief to the patient. The next task was to gather data that would form a plausible context for his anxiety and help in the identification of the belief system relevant to his symptoms.

Certainly, the majority of time in cognitive therapy is oriented to the *identification of, and then the evaluation of, automatic thoughts*. Once a problem focus is established, how does the therapist guide the patient in "locating" the relevant cognitions? Frequently, the therapist asks questions. These questions may focus on the "meaning" of an event or situation. With a patient who has difficulty identifying cognitions, imagery may be useful. When the patient is directed to picture the situation "as it occurred," associated thoughts may become evident to him or her. Alternatively, mind pictures may be investigated just like automatic thoughts, as elicitors of feelings and behavior.

When the concept of an automatic thought is unclear, asking the patient to recall a strong past emotion and then to search for the thinking associated with it may clarify the matter. If none of the above is successful, role play and role reversal may prompt an awareness of cognitions. Once the problem of "no thoughts" is encountered, a strong case can be made for the patient's keeping a daily log of situations, feelings, and automatic thoughts. This record, maintained between sessions, is often helpful even for patients who can identify cognitions easily. It may bridge the gap of elapsed time effectively and permit the patient to work with you today in terms of yesterday's thoughts. Finally, everyone has cognitions related to the situation of attending and participating in a psychotherapy session. Asking about these may facilitate the patient's understanding of this basic concept.

Once you've identified the automatic thoughts, what next? One approach is to *focus on the errors in thinking* (e.g., personalization, polarization, overgeneralization). This is particularly useful when the patient can become aware of making an error consistently, across a variety of situations. A format to do this involves the use of the *triple column technique*: a listing of situation, feeling, and automatic thought. The patient may keep a memo book that forms the basis for working with automatic thoughts between sessions (on his own), as well as during sessions (with you).

In addition, visual confrontation by means of a blackboard can facilitate sending a double-barreled message to the brain: auditory and visual. The "triple column" may, at a given time, actually consist of as many as five columns: situation, feelings, automatic thoughts, cognitive errors, and alternative responses.

A young woman came to see me shortly after she had separated from her husband of five years. Soon after leaving with her two young children, she had become seriously depressed. She discussed the three reasons that summarized why she had left. She believed that these needs, which had gone unmet, warranted her leaving the marriage and "trying again." I asked her to pinpoint the meanings related to leaving that might underlie the depression. I then formed three columns on the blackboard and wrote her responses in the third column under *Thoughts* (see Figure 4).

I then asked her to check the logic of her thinking, to see if it made sense or if there was an error. She believed that her first thought assigned responsibility for her husband's happiness to her. Since she felt that she had adequate reasons to leave, it seemed unreasonable for her to shoulder all the blame. She felt her second thought represented a jump to an unsupportable conclusion. Her last thought reminded her of mother's cautions to her when she was younger. Mother frequently told her what she "should" do. In a fourth column, I noted the errors in her thinking (see Figure 5).

Finally, we worked together to develop alternatives. She felt that she deserved some responsibility for leaving her husband; however, it would be up to him to choose a life path for himself. She would try to support him in this effort. She realized that she could not predict that path from the facts now available. He may choose to remain "alone," or he may over time form new relationships. Since she believed that her reasons for leaving were valid, a

FIGURE 4: TRIPLE COLUMN TECHNIQUE

Situation	Feeling(s)	Thoughts
left husband	sad, depressed	1. My husband doesn't want me to leave. It's my fault that he's unhappy.
		2. He will probably have to live the rest of his life alone.
		3. A loving wife would stay with a man who loved her.

FIGURE 5: TRIPLE COLUMN TECHNIQUE

Situation	Feeling(s)	Thoughts	Errors
		1.	1. Personalization
		2.	2. Arbitrary inference
		3.	3. Should statement

man's love alone did not constitute sufficient reason to stay. I wrote the alternatives in a fifth column on the blackboard (see Figure 6).

How much of this work is done in the office and how much between sessions depends upon the patient's capacity. The same person, with diminishing anxiety or depression, may do increasing amounts of the work by him or herself, using the sessions to review work with the therapist. The objective is to teach the method, review how well it has been learned, follow up on its use, and then to make yourself available for "booster sessions." There are a variety of ways to challenge distorted automatic thoughts and to generate new conceptualizations. We'll return to these later in this chapter.

Homework assignments may take a variety of forms and be used for a variety of purposes. Patients referred for cognitive therapy generally expect to be assigned homework. An assignment helps to structure and formalize what is expected of the patient outside of the office. Together, you may anticipate an upcoming situation and prepare the patient to analyze it in a future session. Homework may also help in teaching the concept of the automatic thought.

FIGURE 6: TRIPLE COLUMN TECHNIQUE

Situation	Feeling(s)	Thoughts	Errors	Alternatives
				1. He must take responsibility for himself.
				2. I can't predict his future.
				3. A partner's love is not enough.

A common cognitive technique used early in psychotherapy involves the *separation of the uncontrollable from the controllable.* Depressed and anxious patients frequently hold themselves accountable for *outcomes.* It is useful to point out that we cannot control outcomes, only devise alternative approaches if the result is not satisfactory. I sometimes make the analogy of giving a large party and worrying about the effect of a rainy day. Whether or not it will rain on a given day cannot generally be controlled (even its *prediction* is often not made with accuracy!). A depressed patient is apt to say, "If it rains, the party will be ruined. And, as my luck goes, it probably will rain." The arbitrary inference (jump to a conclusion) inherent in this formulation can be pointed out to the patient. The overgeneralization ("my luck . . . rain") can be noted as well. Then, I may call the patient's attention to "rain" as an uncontrollable factor. Often, however, provisions can be made (covering the party area, alternative date, bringing people inside the house) to deal with this uncontrollable contingency. Wonderful parties have been given despite the rain. When the "uncontrollable" comes up in a different context later on, I remind the patient, "You remember, you can't control the rain . . . "

BREAKING THE SET

Beck[24] has used the term "cognitive set" to describe a person's immediate state of mind. This designation encompasses the rules (schemas), as well as the attitudes and expectations (cognitions, automatic thoughts), that comprise an individual's belief system. One generalization identifies the "negative cognitive set" of the depressed patient. Another might describe the anxious patient's belief system as one of "controlling the present and anticipating the future." In a patient with anger as a dominant theme, the cognitive set may center upon "the collection of injustices."

Once the relevant beliefs and rules have been identified, cognitive therapy proceeds into its second phase. The aim of the collaborating, problem-solving team is now to "break the set." It has been suggested[28] that, in the emotional disorders, a person's thinking becomes frozen in place. He or she applies (uncritically) the same stereotyped meanings to a wide range of situations and events, as well as to him or herself. The task is to "unfreeze" or dislodge these beliefs from their autonomous state and to subject them to the patient's inquiry. I sometimes refer to this process clinically as "putting your ideas on the table," so that both patient and therapist can work with them.

Three ways to break the set involve the use of *analogies*, the power of *self-disclosure*, and the liberating potential of *humor*. Taken together, their success requires the engagement of the patient in the "story" that the therapist tells. With each technique, the relevance of the intervention to the problem being discussed is usually kept implicit. The patient's task is first to " make the jump" from his or her set to that of the protagonist in the story. Second, he or she must make the connection (see the relevance) of the story to the problem being discussed. Finally, the patient must come to some conclusion about the material presented and then, switching back to his own cognitive set, apply that conclusion to his or her own belief system. When this works, the patient will be led to examine more objectively one tenet of his or her own thinking. There are perils at every step, and the therapist must be prepared to guide, prod, actively challenge, or gently support the patient, as his or her instinct and experience dictate.

A patient presented the following problem. "Every time I have an intimate relationship with a man," she said, "I find a way to ruin it. It's because I'm damaged. I'm damaged by the effect my childhood had on me, and the devastating impact of my divorce. I try really hard to please a man so that he'll commit himself to me. But, they never do.

"When they don't comply with or anticipate a simple request or need, I get angry and feel failed. When the anger builds, I become convinced that they don't really love me. At that point, either the man leaves me or I decide to end the relationship. Either way, men seem to me to be miserable creatures and I end up alone again, proving to myself that I will never be loved. Most women I know get married and stay married. Some are less attractive than I am. Some are not very bright. A few are downright obnoxious. But, they're chosen and I'm not. What's wrong with me?"

There are many errors in thinking illustrated here. This woman saw herself as a "prisoner of her past" with little choice available to her in the here-and-now. Most clinicians have seen this formulation in one of its many guises. Her schema requiring that she please a man, regardless of the consequences, is one she could not yet view objectively. It prohibited her from expressing a small anger.

Generalizations followed, with a resultant buildup of anger. The generalizations reinforced her negative self-view, which helped maintain a state of chronic depression. Another set of generalizations defined "all men as alike." Whether she took action to end the relationship or was the "passive recipient of being rejected," she concluded that she had failed again. The meaning of an acute failure reinforced her ongoing self-image as damaged or defective.

The task for the therapy now is neither to "cure" her nor to approach all of her cognitive errors in one fell swoop. Rather, the therapist will attempt, by means of an analogy, to target a critical assumption and encourage her to look at it more objectively. Once the negative cognitive set has begun to unravel, there will be more opportunities to attack its other aspects.

I heard her explication of the problem over several sessions. I thought about how I might demonstrate to her the errors (so apparent to me) in her thinking. Suddenly, the words of a popular song came to mind. Unfortunately, popular music was not this woman's favorite, but I was willing to bet she could overcome that and would hear a personal message in the lyric. I began:

"There is a song, popular now especially among the kids, called *Paradise by the Dashboard Light*. It's recorded by a man who calls himself Meatloaf. (We each grinned at this.) It doesn't speak to you directly, but I'd like you to listen to it, and I'd be interested in your reaction." I played the tape through from the beginning to the end. The song presents an adolescent boy and girl in a parked car. He can "see paradise by the dashboard light." She is more reluctant to get involved in lovemaking with him. The song abruptly shifts into an allegorical baseball game, broadcast by the old New York Yankee radioman, Phil Rizzuto. This portion concretizes the notion of "scoring" by following a runner on the bases. As he heads for home plate, the baseball allegory ends and the story line returns to the two protagonists.

Now, the woman beseeches her male friend: "Will you love me forever, for the rest of your life? Will you never leave me? Will you make me your wife?" He responds, "I'll give you my answer in the morning." The rhythm and tone of the song build to a number of climaxes, as the dialogue becomes more urgent. He finally promises to "love you 'til the end of time." At the end, both lament that they are now "praying for the end of time, so I can end my time with you." Tough stuff. And not recommended unless the trust in the relationship is such that the patient won't feel humiliated by the implications she may draw from your presentation of the song.

The song ended. I turned off the tape. She made the transition quickly from the situation of the song, the youthful age of the participants, and the off-putting (to her) rock beat, to her own system of meanings. "Do you think I come across that screechingly about commitment?" she said. "And maybe that, plus my overwhelming efforts to please, drives some men away." Her cognitive system relevant to relating to a man opened, just a bit. Over subsequent months, she found some alternative strategies. She became confident enough to risk a relationship again. She slid back and then advanced slowly forward. She ended a relationship prematurely and then allowed it to resume. It was clear, both to her and to me, that some basic attitudes had changed. This was accompanied by a change to a less depressed, more optimistic state of both thinking and feeling.

The preceding is a fairly dramatic use of an analogy to unfreeze a cognitive set. Usually, a story about a friend, a recollection from the past, or the mention of a current news article makes for a gentler analogy. Whether the analogy is dramatically presented or not, however, the cognitive process is still the same.

Self-disclosure works in a way similar to that described for analogies. This time, the analog comes from the therapist's life, his or her own family, his or her own life experience. The clinical prohibition against self-revelation has frequently prevented psychotherapists from using this approach. And, it *is* fraught with dangers. As with the more general analogy, it may be seen by the patient as irrelevant and a waste of time in therapy. It may be seen as lecturing ("a Johnny Carson monologue") or worse—as something done purely for the therapist's own gratification. Once again, the trusting nature of the relationship must provide the context within which it can succeed.

Once the caveats are identified and honored, however, one of the most unexpected gifts a therapist can confer upon a patient is a glimpse into his or her own life, given for the patient's benefit. For this, we can thank the psychoanalytic tradition, which leads most patients to expect little if any self-revelation by the therapist. The active collaborative quality of the relationship in cognitive therapy forms an effective framework for the successful use of self-disclosure.

For example, a patient recently eased out of a job was confronting the meanings and consequences of unemployment and job-seeking. I listened first to the explication of his concerns. Then I told him the following story. "It's a very real problem that you're talking about," I said, "and I should know. Several years ago, I was told that I would be dismissed from an academic position four months from the date of receipt of a termination letter. I was angry and bitter initially, much as you were. Then, I became saddened and began to doubt myself. I could not then look for another job. Friends and colleagues rallied, initially, to what they saw as unjust treatment. Then a curious thing happened. People began crossing the street when I came walking down. I believed they were saying that I was part of the past and, although they sympathized, they wanted to be part of the future. The four months of working but not being really a part of the system were very difficult for me. I gather that you've felt just that for months now. It was a great relief to finally get out of there. The bigger relief for me, though, was to separate what had happened to me from the meanings I had given to it. When you're ready to, I hope I can guide you through the disengagement process."

This acutely depressed man nodded and smiled gently through my short monologue. He then cried, grew angry, and then began to test some of the self-assumptions he had earlier outlined. A point of contact had been established, and an approach to his problem had begun.

In addition to relating my own experience, I tell some stories "on my wife," but I'm convinced that the most engaging interventions concern the problem–solving pitfalls and pratfalls of my two, now adolescent kids. A carefully told story of a child can be surprisingly applicable to the life situation and meanings of an adult.

Another powerful tool, which must be thoughtfully applied to succeed in opening a frozen cognitive set, involves the *use of humor*. Some cautions have been discussed by Beck.[4] For humor to be effective, it must fit the therapist's style. It must be presented with spontaneity. If you do this with difficulty in social situations among friends, this technique is *not* for you. The goal is to illustrate the unreasonableness (distortion) in the patient's thinking.

Humor must challenge a key element in the patient's belief system. Be aware that, particularly by the depressed patient, it may not be heard as intended. It must avoid ridicule. Often, it helps if it's self-deprecating, although some depressed patients will immediately see themselves as the remark's victim. Once the joke or witty remark is made, the procedure is identical to that outlined for the use of analogy or self-disclosure. The patient must abstract the relevant element and apply it to him or herself. The form of the remark may be a quip, a rapid-fire response to a question, or a short story.

WORKING WITH AUTOMATIC THOUGHTS

We've now come to the cusp between cognitive therapy's second and third phases. The following work with automatic thoughts is aimed at breaking the set and then at initiating the process of generating alternative meanings. It provides one answer to the question: "What do you do after you've identified relevant automatic thoughts?" Along with our triple column technique (situation, feeling, automatic thought), we now focus on a fourth category, "cognitive error." Similar errors made in high frequency are identified and general alternative conceptualizations may be offered to personalization, polarization, and overgeneralization.

Evidence may be collected for and against the patient's chosen meaning. An experiment may be proposed to test the validity of a key assumption. The patient may be urged to compare his or her view with those of significant others or friends ("polling"). Often a belief is tested by continually questioning its consequences. This is referred to as the "So–What Question" or the "Downward Arrow Technique."[29]

An anxious physician patient described an incident of becoming aware of testicular pain while showering. He had become suddenly flushed and felt faint; he remained preoccupied with the meaning of the pain for days. He had decided not to consult a urologist about it, rather to discuss it with me. "After I felt this pain," he said, "I gingerly touched the area that hurt and felt something hard, like a lump. I thought, 'This is a tumor. Most tumors of the testicle are malignant. Maybe I will die. At best, I'll need surgery and be out of commission for a long time. How will my family survive without my income? I should have bought that disability insurance. There is no way that this story can have a benign ending. Even if the tumor is benign, it will, at least, have to be biopsied. Then I'll be laid up for a long time and out of work. Maybe if I forget about it, it will go away.'"

His assumptions were outlined on the blackboard, with arrows linking one to the next. I asked him to subject his logic to reality-testing. He had left no room for a benign outcome. With prodding, he found one. "Years ago, I had a vasectomy," he said, "and maybe, somehow this lump is related to it. Moreover, if I wait and it's malignant, I may be signing a death warrant. I don't want to stop working, but, I guess, that would be preferable to killing myself by trying to avoid this."

A consultation that afternoon with a urologist confirmed the most benign outcome. It was a thickened spermatic cord, a direct result of the vasectomy he had 13 years earlier which had escaped notice over the ensuing years.

In summary, the middle stage of cognitive therapy is occupied with the task of breaking the frozen cognitive set encountered in many emotional disorders. Analogy, self-disclosure, and humor, as well as various techniques to challenge automatic thoughts, prepare the patient for the psychotherapy's final stage: the generation of alternative meanings.

GENERATING ALTERNATIVES

To this point cognitive therapy, although not identical to psychodynamic psychotherapy, has followed a parallel path. Distortions have been identified as such, and the meanings that have served as obstacles have largely been removed from the road leading to change. The relationship has served to provide a trusting, accepting, and genuine context, within which learning can be facilitated. At this point, however, cognitive therapy's path diverges sharply from that of traditional therapy. Insight–oriented treatment usually ends here, anticipating that the patient will cover the distance from making connections and removing obstacles to changing by him or herself. Paradoxically, it is the *short-term* therapy that moves into a final phase, guiding the patient to achieve the change he has sought.

In order to change, one must specify some options to "change to." I don't believe that the source of these alternatives is significant. It may be the patient him or herself. It may be the therapist (a collaborating partner). It may be the suggestion of a significant other. It may be the result of reading a book.

The only source for alternatives that may require a bit of elaboration is the therapist. Some patients will invest a therapist's suggestions with the authority of law. They may comply, with little attention paid to their own thoughts and feelings. If the therapist's suggestions prove to be of little value, they may be reluctant to say so. They may, conversely, blame and derogate the therapist or the therapy. It is important, therefore, to clarify the rules of the model, so that the therapist can contribute freely to the generation of alternatives. I often reemphasize to the patient at this point that, if I am to feel free to toss out ideas, he or she must give my contributions to *this* portion of therapy the *same* consideration given to contributions from other sources—no more and no less.

One generic label for this final therapeutic task is *reattribution or reframing techniques*. To each situation, event, or relationship, a person applies a meaning or "makes an attribution." When this meaning has outlived its usefulness, an attempt is made to reattribute or to view the circumstance in a different frame or context.

Techniques to generate alternatives may be understood with

regard to the cognitive error made in reaching the initial conclusion. If the error is personalization, the task is to *decenter*.[22] I might use the metaphor of a television screen to explain the task to the patient. "When you reached the (distorted) conclusion, you placed yourself in the center of the screen. The outcome was expressed with you as its focus. Now, try to remove yourself from the screen, refocus, and tell me what else you see."

If the error is polarization, the task is to generate "grays" or *middle-ground alternatives*. Most judgments need not be black or white. "You may not achieve 100% on your exam, but neither may you fail utterly. What would represent a 90% response? An 80% response?"

If the patient is so enmeshed or absorbed in the immediacy of a situation that the meaning is distorted, sometimes *perspective training*[22] will lead to the identification of alternatives. Consider a man in his mid-twenties who has lost a prized relationship. In its wake, he may see himself as having failed. He may expect to "never love again." He may believe that he lacks an essential element to be loved. I ask the patient to add 40 years to his age, for a moment. "Picture yourself as 65 years old, looking back upon this event as though it happened 40 years ago. Do you think that Susan will be the main topic of your book of life? Will she make up one chapter? Will she be relegated, perhaps, to a mere footnote? Will she be cited in the index?" Sometimes, this shift of set to "capture the wisdom of aging" helps the patient to regain some lost perspective.

When the cognitive error is overgeneralization, an attempt is made to make the patient account for his conclusion by specifying the data that support it. Since we learn by making (accurate) generalizations, this process is not discouraged. Rather, the illogic of accepting a related but unsupportable conclusion (overgeneralization) is challenged. If you have loved and lost (for example) because of a need or action of someone else, that event has little power to predict the outcome of your subsequent relationships with others. If you have lost due to a need or action of your own, perhaps an inquiry is indicated that will identify this pattern and suggest alternatives to you. Successful self-change can alter or remove the power of a negative prediction of the future.

Visual confrontation techniques (e.g., the triple column) have their usefulness, once again, in this phase of therapy. Now the focus turns to the "fifth column" (alternative responses), with the other four designations (situation, feelings, automatic thoughts, cognitive errors) serving as a context and as prompts. Once again, the work may be done during the session or assigned as homework.

Homework assignments may take a variety of forms. The patient or therapist may propose an experiment designed to develop alternative approaches to a problem. I once treated a young woman who was capable and competent in a variety of ways, despite her chronic suffering with depression. Her mother's weekly telephone call was a time of unparalleled stress for her and usually led to a torrent of negative self-appraisals. She was told that she was "a bad wife, a horrible mother, an unskilled homemaker." It became clear that these assessments formed the basis for her own negative overgeneralizations, which could be seen as maintaining her depression. The task was to help her view the situation of "the phone call" more objectively. She had become part of a dyadic event with her mother that had serious negative consequences for herself.

"I have a little experiment I'd like you to try as homework," I told her. "It may seem silly at first, but I wonder if you'd be willing to do it? The next time mother calls, I want you to say 'hello' and then make that the last word you utter, until it's time to say goodbye. You may listen to mother, twirl the phone on its cord, or even lay it down briefly and come back." Reluctantly (the request made little sense to her), she promised me that she would try it.

When she returned in a week, I asked her if she had done the experiment (she had) and what she had learned. "I want you to know," she said,"that it seemed like a dumb idea to me. Well, mother called and I said 'Hi' and then said nothing more. She talked on and on, for 20 minutes! I have always thought that she was responding to me, but this time she didn't seem to need my help. She posed questions and answered them. It felt like I was really *listening* to her for the first time. Some of what she said was ridiculous—but some of it made sense. I was tempted to argue back, but I said nothing. I felt an odd sense of mastery afterwards that I don't usually feel when we are together. I began to consider this phone call business as 'her act' being done to meet 'her need.' I'm not as sure that 'my traits' play a real part in it after all."

Some time later, mother came for a visit. On the patient's instruction, her husband joined her in trying harder to observe mother more and to participate less, within the bounds of courtesy and caring. The patient found herself, on several occasions, suppressing a giggle at statements mother made that used to trouble her greatly. It seemed that she had managed to reframe the meaning of some of mother's talk. She reported feeling far more relaxed with mother and capable of "enjoying her" at home for the first time.

Another technique for generating alternatives is particularly useful in sensitizing an indecisive patient to the factors affecting his or her decision-making. This is variously referred to as a cost-benefit analysis[29] or a *balance sheet*. Simply put, the therapist lists on a blackboard the assets and liabilities, the pluses and minuses, or the costs and benefits inherent in opting for a particular alternative. I have worked with several couples on issues relevant to infertility using this technique.

The prototype is a recently married couple in their middle to late thirties. They want to have a family and have been trying to conceive for three years. He has endured the psychologically difficult procedure of having his sperm tested for number, motility, and endurance by ejaculating into a test tube. She has endured a lengthy and fruitless workup to uncover which part of her reproductive anatomy is failing the task of providing an egg at the proper time for fertilization. They each feel more like experimental subjects than like deserving parents.

The next phase of this mentally torturous process involves the prescription of drugs for the woman to "enhance her fertility." She has suffered for a year with the disabling side effects. As a couple, they are frustrated and "at the end of their rope." Sexual relations, initially an anticipated pleasure and a source of comfort, have been converted to a means of conception that require planning and measurement. Always, now, sex is associated with a sense of failure and inadequacy. "Anyone can have a child, but we cannot," they each tell themselves. The alternative of adoption is presented to them by her gynecologist. Since neither is comfortable with this option, they consult me for help.

After the history is taken, they make it clear that neither, at this point, is interested in exploratory psychotherapy. They want me to help them make a decision about adoption and then they will go on their way. Together, we form a balance sheet and write the various pros and cons on the blackboard. If they were to adopt a child, they could be parents and start a family. They could terminate this frustrating attempt to conceive naturally. They could return to "normal" sexual functioning. They could end this preoccupation with conception and move on to other life concerns. They might be able, once again, to enjoy one another. They could "be in the same room with" couples who talk incessantly about their own children, without feeling uncomfortable.

But, adopting a child would mean that the biological parents would be someone other than themselves. The baby's genetic traits would have their origin elsewhere. She would forfeit the experience of carrying and delivering a child. The child might have a serious medical problem. It might be cold and distant from each of them. It would resemble neither of them. There might be trouble instigated by the child's biological mother. She cannot be certain that she could ever feel that an adopted child was "hers."

We isolate, together, those statements that represent clear distortions of reality (for example, that the adopted child had a greater chance of having a birth defect than would a naturally born child). They "dispute" with each other, and with me, the validity and importance of the various pros and cons. Over about a six–week period, they make the decision to adopt. They investigate and discuss with me the various options for finding a baby and qualifying for adoption.

We terminate therapy and they keep me informed of their progress. In several cases, I have the pleasure of receiving an announcement of the baby's arrival. In each case, some ambivalence about the procedure has persisted. Each couple who has chosen to adopt, however, has seemed to be pleased overall by the outcome. Several couples have commented about how they "grew together" during the decision-making process.

Bibliotherapy is the formal term for recommending a book.

Since risktaking is a common issue dealt with in my office, I frequently suggest that my patients read David Viscott's book, *Risking*.[30] To expose a new patient painlessly to the cognitive method, I frequently recommend David Burns' book, *Feeling Good*.[29] When the concept of choice is a difficult one to teach, I have given patients a copy of *Illusions: Confessions of a Reluctant Messiah* by Richard Bach.[31]

A TYPICAL COGNITIVE
THERAPY HOUR

Now that we have reviewed the three stages in a cognitive therapy (providing structure and mastery, breaking the set, and generating alternatives), let's look at an individual session. Some time (just a few minutes) at the beginning of the hour is set aside for socialization. This is kibbitz time—time to make the transition from the anticipation of the patient in the parking lot prior to the hour to the therapeutic work to be done in the office. If homework has been assigned, it is critical to go over it. Forgetting it will markedly diminish compliance with future assignments. The approach to homework undone is similar to that with any problem or situation. First, identify the cognitions relevant to the task. Then note the cognitive errors involved and develop alternatives.

The next agenda item is to develop the problem focus for the session. A patient may say," You do the therapy today." At times, it is profitable to explore the meaning of this statement. Has the treatment no clear direction? Is the patient disengaged? Is control an issue being negotiated? At other times, I may suggest some unfinished business from our last meeting, taking the request at face value. After checking to make sure that the patient in fact has no particular plan for the session, I may suggest one. Most often, however, the patient specifies the problem focus. The cognitive work may entail gathering background details, identifying automatic thoughts and cognitive errors, proposing experiments, challenging cognitions or schemas, or generating alternative ways to view a problem.

As the cognitive work draws to a close, homework may be assigned, and often a summary is made of the hour's content. Periodically, progress is assessed with regard to the goals set at the outset and the time elapsed since we began. When an agenda is successfully completed, a new one may be agreed upon. At the end of a successful short-term therapy, sometimes a contract is made for long-term work, dealing largely with the identification and modification of schemas.

Termination considers whether and how change occurred and lays the groundwork for future sessions and the availability of the therapist. When there has been a mismatch between therapist and patient, an early session may consider referral options. When no (or insufficient) progress has been made, termination and referral to a different therapist and/or a different model are considered.

SOME FAMILIAR ALTERNATIVE RESPONSES

I will close this chapter on technique by quoting some punch lines from a noted psychotherapist, philosopher, and author, Sheldon Kopp.[32] These are offered as rational (or alternative) responses to frequently distorted automatic thoughts. See if you can identify the automatic thought and the related cognitive error while you enjoy some thoughtful statements about life situations:

1. Often things *are* as bad as they seem.
2. Why grieve, when nothing helps? We cry *because* nothing helps.
3. What's a person to do about feeling helpless? For a while, there's just no way to see what's funny about being stuck.
4. You can *so* stand it.
5. I have never begun an important venture for which I felt adequately prepared.
6. Not everything worth doing is worth doing well.
7. There's just no way to get it all straight. Mistakes are inevitable.
8. If we allow pain more of our attention than it requires, we miss some opportunities for joy.
9. Escape is not a dirty word. None of us can face what is happening head–on, all of the time.

10. It's all right to pretend sometimes. The only danger lies in pretending you are not pretending.
11. There is nothing to figure out. Life is not *about* anything.
12. Remember, we are all in this *alone*. It helps to know that everyone is in the same situation. It helps, but not a whole lot.
13. We insist that our situation is special. It's so hard to accept how ordinary we all are.
14. By now, I'm no longer interested in whether or not someone *really* loves me. I'll settle for being treated well.
15. We must be willing to go on caring, even when we are helpless to change things.
16. Our best may not turn out to be good enough. Still, it will have to do.
17. I'm not O.K. You're not O.K. . . . and, that's O.K.

III
Applying
the Model

6

In Love—Out of Love

The loss of a loved person is a frequently cited precipitant for acute emotional disorders, particularly depression. In this chapter, we will discuss the state of "being in love," using a cognitive theoretical model as a guide. Then, utilizing this framework, we will consider its impact and the reparative work necessary to help the patient who is "out of love."

IN LOVE

Most of us have experienced the "state of being in love" either personally or through the vehicle of a vivid description by another. Typically, it begins when one person encounters another in a particular situation, often recorded in memory in great detail. A series of contacts ensues in which there may take place the sharing of information about oneself and the learning of the "history" of another. Or, this may not occur. Common interests are identified and often pursued. This may not occur either. Feelings may be discussed and shared. This, too, seems optional.

And then, "it" happens, either with troublesome suddenness or gradual awareness. An affective state supervenes that I will call "being in love." For some, this emotional state is so powerful that it seems to determine its cognitive and behavioral accompaniments. The objective capacity to view one's behavior and, more significant here, to test the validity of one's thinking may be lost. Instead, the behavioral and cognitive apparatuses are recruited to support the affective state.

Before moving on to understand better the cognitive aspects and changes, let me pause and emphasize the power of this affective state. It may totally envelop one's thoughts and feelings and pave the way for some most unusual behavior. It may become the single most important determinant of how one thinks and acts. The critical capacity to judge someone else's behavior as well as one's own may be dominated by the central assumption: "I am in love and nothing can change that. Nothing else matters to me."

The potential for cognitive distortion is significant, particularly in one's view of the loved person. Negative attributes may be discounted or attributed to a cause that leaves the object of love unblemished. It may become (inordinately) important to find out what the object of your love thinks (and feels) about you. Contact with the loved person becomes unreasonably valued. Some search for the person everywhere, hoping for the "surprise of a chance encounter," setting themselves up for the disappointment felt when no such encounter occurs. Understanding the behavior of the loved person tends to be personalized favorably toward the self. In sum, the cognitive system is programmed to perpetuate the affective state.

Culturally, we support the cognitive distortions and sometimes the unusual behavior of the individual in love. We say, "Love is blind," and "Lovers know no reason," to excuse the cognitive errors made. Often the loved person is made a part of one's system of gratification or system of self-worth. Some people have a history of doing this with multiple relationships in sequence. For others, it may happen only once.

OUT OF LOVE

If you have followed the development of the argument so far or, better still, if you have a referent in your life or that of another to make the discussion more meaningful, you should now be prepared for the denouement. In a variety of possible ways, the loved person makes it clear to you that he (or she) does not share your love (anymore?).

Often, this acknowledgment is greeted by one's belief system as a lie, perpetrated for a purpose. With repetition and/or behavior to support it, the statement cries out to be believed. And now, the losses begin to multiply. The "space" occupied by the loved person is vacated. The meaning attributed to that person's loving is lost.

To the extent that the loved person was made part of some judgment of the self, this self-appraisal may be in danger of sudden devaluation. Common affects experienced include sadness at the loss of love and anger directed either at the loved one (for spurning the love offered) or at the self (for having made a mistaken interpretation of another's feelings). For some, a more significant loss is the termination of the "state of being" in love.

The lover's cognitive set may range in any of several directions. With the persistence of the highly valued status of the loved one, despite his or her withdrawal, the self may be devalued. In the face of anger directed at the loved one who has left, he or she may also be devalued. Various expectations are raised, considered in the light of the lover's own beliefs, and often go unmet. Disappointment and anger may be potentiated in this way, with no further input from the loved one. The power of the "state of being" may be such that the belief is raised that, "I shall never feel this way about anyone again." Or, "Nothing works out well for me." The lover mourns for the loss of the loved one, often for the loss of a part of the self, and for the lost state of extreme well-being.

Deliberate changes in behavior or attempts to manipulate the affects are of little use. My thesis is that the bereaved state of the forsaken lover is maintained by his or her beliefs. The need is for cognitive restructuring, whether undertaken by oneself or with the help of a psychotherapist. Attention is profitably paid to several areas: the lover's view of him or herself, the achievement of a more rational view of the significant other, and an examination of the consequences of the love relationship and its termination.

The lover may be plagued by a constant media (radio, magazine) barrage about "being in love" or "losing a love." One patient told me that he could not listen to the radio station in my waiting room, since he felt it emphasized songs on these themes. Paradoxically, for the person more distant from feelings, the mourning process may be aided by exposure to material evoking anger or sadness related to loving.

The "state of being in love" may form a delicious memory to keep (which no one can ever take away). Being in love and losing a love may provide a framework for growth and substantial self-awareness. The resolution of the state of bereavement and its preoccupation (parallel to the preoccupation of being in love) may bring great relief and the gift of time and freedom. However, if it is permitted to wash constantly over the self, it may erode self-worth, lead to social withdrawal, and diminish trust and the willingness to risk.

THE COGNITIVE WORK

The treatment of this problem begins with the provision of a framework within which the patient can view him or herself and the situation. I have found the concept of *forming an illusion or icon* to be a simple, useful, and vivid way to approach the problem of a patient who has lost a lover.

I discuss with the patient how the process of falling in love results in the production of an icon (much like the little box on a computer screen), which represents the sum total of his beliefs about his beloved. This icon is elaborated over time as new *positive* data are admitted uncritically and *negative* data are routinely blocked from gaining access. It becomes a growing hymn to the beauty, the wonder, and the value of the loved person. Negative input, whether from friends or from appraisals generated by the lover him or herself is discounted, denied, or explained away. When the rejection occurs, the starting point for the grieving process that follows is rarely the reality of the person or opportunity that has been lost. Rather it is the icon, that collection of positively biased beliefs, that must be contested before an eventual meaning can be given to the relationship and a place can be found for it that is compatible with the resumption of life's tasks and pleasures. And so, the cognitive work divides into three phases:

1. Challenge the icon.
2. Dismantle the icon.
3. Reformulate a self-view that incorporates the relationship experience but permits the formation of new links and the experiencing of pleasure.

Initially, the patient and I often discuss the acquisition of beliefs and expectations about the loved person. Then, inconsistencies are identified between what the icon predicts and what the patient has observed. This process may go on for a lengthy period of time as the patient (who claims that he or she ought to know better) continues to apply the expectancies of the icon to drive thinking, feelings, and behavior. Once freed of this framework, the patient has the task of returning to a cognitive set that existed prior to the relationship or of growing from the experience and reformulating a self-view that is "wiser" for having known the loved person. If the outcome fits a pattern of lost relationships, the identification of the distorted meanings involved can pave the way for meaningful changes that may affect the outcome of future relationships.

Whether the pairing is heterosexual or homosexual, the task and process seem to be the same. A middle-aged man consulted me after the loss of a younger male lover. Faced with clues to the impending end of the relationship, my patient "tried to be the person his lover wanted him to be." He shifted his values to accept the infidelities of his partner. He emphasized their age difference as a major reason for his lover's leaving. He became preoccupied with the importance of somehow "saving" the relationship and with the "impossibility" of accepting its demise.

He believed that he would never love again, citing the claim that, in homosexual society especially, the premium placed upon youth would severely limit his attractiveness and the opportunity to meet someone else. He feared sexual impotence. He anticipated additional rejections. He wanted to "surgically remove" his grief so that he could begin living again. Simultaneously, he felt that he would grieve forever. He began to demand constant reassurance from friends and from me. He talked about a loss of pride. He had begun to drink while alone.

We adopted several strategies. First, he was to initiate no further contact with his lover. Second, he was to orient himself to involvement with friends, work, and personal tasks. Third, he was to keep a triple column log, detailing feelings, situations, and automatic thoughts. Fourth, he was continually to relate his positive urgings for his lover to the illusion (icon) and check their basis in reality before acting on them. Fifth, our cognitive work in sessions would focus on the log that he maintained for homework.

Typically a "stay at home" and intensely private individual, he found the shift toward taking more social initiative and engaging in more goal-directed activity difficult. Initially, there was a flood of negative overgeneralizations about the future. By the two-month mark, there was some adaptive behavior that enabled a more optimistic prediction about the future. He began to detach the relationship from other life decisions, like where to live and work. He bought a car and took a vacation. A letter from his old lover sparked a brief downturn, but his uncharacteristically assertive response limited the reaction to a short time. He became more and more capable of going out alone and more socially involved with a large group of friends.

The holiday season proved to be another stressor for him. He recognized that the "icon was still speaking to him," despite its having been quiet now for several months. Many of his anticipations for Christmas had been linked with places, thoughts, and feelings of his lost love. It took nearly 10 months for him to feel comfortable living alone in his new place. By then, the preoccupation was gone and he could see that others "have as many problems as I do." The last six months of therapy focused on the issue of liking himself and the relevant schemas. This had been a lifelong problem, whose resolution now had a new urgency. At termination, he felt that he had indeed utilized the event of a lost love as a springboard for growth.

In this case, a relationship had developed over years, accommodations had been made to the wants and habits of each partner, and multiple common interests were pursued together. Arbitrary inferences and overgeneralizations were the orders of the day, as my patient accepted uncritically his negative self-prognosis and was certain that he would never love again. Furthermore, all that a relationship can bring would be forever foreclosed to him. He was angry at having to surrender "life as a couple" to return to living as a single man. Finally, he blamed himself for the outcome, confirming a lifelong self-view of inadequacy. Because he shared a community of friends with his lover, he would now be confronted with "his failure" wherever he went. He could anticipate the difficulty of seeing his partner with future lovers. Some have experienced this phenomenon in a relationship between coworkers. When the relationship ends, all must coexist "within the same, small space" or someone must leave. Certainly, the task of grieving a lost love still alive and open to new partners is more difficult than mourning the death of a loving partner.

Or is it? The next example will challenge the logic that loss by death is always "easier" to overcome than rejection in life. An older woman was referred to me because she could not accept the death of her husband of 30 years, which had occurred 10 years earlier. In her view, his love and acceptance of her maintained her self-worth. Without him, she felt worthless. She traveled, knew many people, had multiple opportunities, but she enjoyed nothing and was frequently suicidal and continuously depressed. She felt rejected by her three grown sons and one daughter, rootless in her life, and "always alone."

It seemed that the icon she had constructed for her husband was virtually impregnable. The therapeutic work consisted, therefore, of challenging the choice of continuing to see herself in terms of her husband, instead of formulating a separate self-view. By the ninth session (four months after therapy had begun), she was able to consider the choices she had instead of perseverating on the tragic consequences of her loss. She was able to see her role in making her children's time with her difficult for them. She opened the door, ever so slightly, to the possibility of a new relationship. "It could never replace my marriage," she said, supporting the validity of the icon, "but it would be nice to have someone in my life again."

As luck sometimes will have it, she was introduced to a man just as she seemed to be preparing herself to look forward instead of backward. She was ready to present herself to him in a positive and optimistic fashion. Major changes in her thinking about herself, her family, and the future were evident. Ten months had elapsed from the onset of therapy and nearly 11 years from her husband's death.

Yet another pattern involves the long-term, committed relationship that ends with one partner's leaving the other. Heterosexual society identifies this as a marital breakup after many years together. Among homosexuals, once again, the issues are little different. A man in his mid-forties came to see me because his relationship of 20 years was breaking up, and he was depressed and in crisis. Each partner had been involved in extra–marital relationships, but each time the marriage had survived. Now his mate was citing a lack of support for a burgeoning career. My patient's symptoms included sleep difficulty, crying spells, overeating, withdrawal, extreme fatigue, and an exaggerated tendency to self-blame. He felt hurt, angry, and sad.

A collateral session with his marital partner, a man five years younger than the patient, was consistent with the patient's view of the relationship terminating. The patient felt deserted. He would now have to live alone. How could he explain the loss to their friends? Possessions would have to be divided. He would "grow old alone." In sessions, he would suddenly burst out crying. However, he had begun to redecorate his lover's room in the house. The anger gave way to depression and a search for meaning.

He dealt first with the task of confronting friends. By formulating a meaning he could convey to others, he felt that his own acceptance would be facilitated. He began to speak out at professional meetings and in social gatherings. He avoided, for now, even casual contact with his former lover. He acknowledged how important it was for him to be a nurturer.

In our sessions together, I explored with him the various facets of his identity. He was a skilled attorney, in considerable demand by clients. He had a love for history, and read (especially books on European history) voraciously. He was a capable tennis player and had a group of "tennis friends." He loved to travel and had traveled extensively. In all four areas, there were social contacts and all the elements for a rich existence. It was important to help him detach the loss of a relationship from his sense of who he was and what he could do. Gradually, he reclaimed those parts of his identity that had little bearing on his partner and their separation. With this accomplished, he had more confidence entering into social situations and meeting new people.

After three months (14 sessions), he mentioned his concern that it would be difficult for him eventually to separate from me. The therapeutic focus was kept on his adaptational issues. The issue of our relationship was not pursued at this point. As he generated, and we tested, beliefs about himself and the consequences of the lost relationship, he centered upon his need for belonging. He was reformulating an identity from the status of "married" to one of "single." He thought about moving, a job change, and buying a vacation home.

Six months into therapy, he began a new relationship. There was a return of "nostalgic feelings" for his old lover. There was a need to validate the many years he had invested in the relationship. He had begun, at last, to let go. He talked about the vulnerability inherent in aging as a single man. He felt that he had to "clean up his inner court" before making a commitment to someone new.

He gave a large party eight months after the loss, and it went well. He felt that he had related easily to many different kinds of people. Finally, we discussed termination and dwelt upon our relationship — but also on what had changed in him, and how he felt that change had occurred. He saw me as a guide, consistent with his interest in history. I was his teacher, a source of support, sharing, and acceptance. He hoped that we could remain friends. He wanted to know more about my professional interests, and we spoke of them. I hear from him still, from time to time. His life, relationships, and career continue to bring him satisfaction.

Young people usually confront the beginnings and endings of relationships at a high frequency. Some learn to see the sorting process as one of multiple guesses and only occasional matches. They often grow with the endings (even though they are painful) and sharpen their notion of the person who would make a good mate. Others view each relationship as an opportunity to succeed or fail, a referendum on whether or not they are worthwhile. Seeing each ending as a rejection and a failure, they sometimes lose the motivation to continue the search. Occasionally they conclude, tragically, that life without a significant other is no longer worth living.

A woman in her mid-twenties consulted me after three months of psychoanalytic psychotherapy, saying that she "needed interaction now." Ten months earlier, a man with whom she had lived for a year, and from whom she had a promise of marriage, left rather abruptly. Four months earlier, she had swallowed a significant number of pills in an attempted suicide. Now, she was having suicidal thoughts again, and a concerned friend had suggested that she seek further help.

She felt that she had never fit in with the other kids at school. There were cliques of smart, attractive, and athletic girls. She saw herself as none of these. In the years that followed school, she had found neither a mate nor a career. What she wanted most now was a return of the "extreme state of happiness" she experienced when she and her lover were together. This is similar to the "state of being in love" referred to earlier in this chapter. In addition, she still "really loved him" and "could not let him go." She felt the loss was "unfair." She felt sorry for herself and spoke about how she had fashioned a whole life plan around the anchor of their relationship. She articulated well how her loss had consisted of "much more than him."

We began to work with her icon. In time, she achieved a more realistic view of her lover, but she could not redirect her attention from the magnitude of her loss and its irreversibility. She had little motivation to pursue either another relationship or a career. In contrast to the first person discussed in this chapter, she found it useful to contact her ex and to continually reappraise his responses to her. He confirmed for her the fear of commitment that led him to break off a relationship as it approached marriage. He confirmed as well that little change was likely for him. This, for her, made for a clear attribution to "his needs" of the reason the relationship ended. After a three–month period in therapy, she affirmed that her involvement with him was now over.

She turned next to tackle a variety of identity issues that had surfaced in the wake of the relationship's end. What did she want for herself? Who was she really? And, what would suit her in a career? These concerns ushered in a year of psychotherapy, with the original focus bubbling up occasionally. For the most part, it appeared to be resolved satisfactorily.

S————7
eparated

As if a lost love wasn't trouble enough, marital separation often complicates the situation by adding problems and multiplying the losses. Separation from a spouse may mean a loss of security, a loss of status, a loss of income, a lost role, lost stability, increased responsibility, as well as the need to function in a singles' environment, for some joyfully abandoned years ago. Particularly when one's self-definition has become centered upon the role of "spouse," marital separation may be an event that threatens self-worth. Feelings of sadness, anxiety, anger, helplessness, and loneliness may become constant companions. These feelings (and the thoughts that are associated with them) may erode the initiative, assertiveness, and self-confidence necessary to form new relationships.

Separation may present itself in other guises, as well. The British (more often than the Americans) speak of "being separated from" (rather than "losing") a job. Here, too, the fundamental loss is often magnified by lost income, status, security, role, and stability. In addition, responsibility to provide for others may be an added burden at this time. The return to functioning in a job-seeking mode is clearly similar to the task of returning to problems of dating and meeting people.

Even when marriage and job are enduring, that stage when grown children leave home may inflict a loss similar to marital and job separation. The "empty nest" may be accompanied by a lost role and lost status, a confrontation between husband and wife as solitary partners again, and a need to redefine purpose and direction in life, particularly when one's self-definition has become centered upon the role of "parent."

COGNITIVE PROBLEMS IN
SEPARATION

When one has walked with a partner by one's side for a variable period of time, the end of a marriage poses the prospect of "facing life alone." A separated woman, married for 20 years and now 40 years old, told me, "I can't see surviving as a single person. I have no status alone. I'm not smart enough. I am afraid without him. I haven't thought of myself in 20 years." A separated woman in her mid-thirties with two small children said, "I feel like I was thrown off a ship in mid-ocean. If he doesn't love me, how can anybody love me?" A separated woman in her mid-thirties was concerned with loneliness, dating again, and financial worries. "His leaving was my fault," she said, "The separation is my failure."

A man in his early thirties, left by his wife, told me, "Her leaving is my fault. I don't really like myself. I feel out of place in a singles' atmosphere." A separated man in his mid-forties said, "I'll never find another woman who will love me. I feel like a boat going in circles because I don't know how to steer. If I become sick, who will take care of me?"

Several men and women focused on the new behaviors they would now need to learn: risk-taking, assertiveness, interpersonal skills, decision–making, independence, learning to find pleasure in being alone. Several men and women feared or experienced a return to old "pain-relieving" habits of substance abuse.

For many, there was the concern that "dating now" was nothing like the behavioral repertoire they had practiced earlier in their lives. Sexual mores had changed, I was told. The risk of sexually transmitted disease had risen dramatically. What was appropriate at 18 surely wasn't possible at 38. For some who married child-hood sweethearts, there had never been a "dating phase" to serve as a model. Some would be "living alone" again; for a few, it would be the first time they had *ever* lived alone (they had moved from parents to roommates to spouse).

When there has been deception, sometimes when a next relationship awaits the leaving spouse, or when animosity dictates an unbalanced financial settlement, the sense of helplessness and anger are doubled. When a sensitive individual has chosen to leave a draining relationship, guilt and fear for the safety of the left spouse may be a reason for seeking therapy.

Complicating the idiosyncratic individual burdens that often accompany separation, society imposes problems and expectations upon the individual, too. These are often presented to me as statements of fact, or at least as consensually validated opinions. "Everyone knows that . . . ," I am told. For example, we live in a paired society. Individuals are rarely invited to dinner unless the occasion is in their honor. Couples are invited by couples. It is less enjoyable to do a wide variety of leisure activities alone. One needs a partner to share the joy. The burdens of life can be nearly intolerable when they are borne alone. Two can divide the chores and lessen the load on each other. It helps to have someone to talk to. It helps to have someone available who cares about you, without your having to make a special arrangement (a date, a telephone call) to secure that person's attention.

"Besides," I am told, "everyone I know is happily married. Why not me?" Treating people in distress, I am in a logical position to hear these arguments. I would guess, however, that most of my readers have heard them as well.

Losing a job can strike similar chords. A man in his late forties was forced out of a job after 20 years of employment. Despite widespread contacts and an admirable reputation as a worker, he felt he lacked the self–confidence to conduct a successful job search. He was highly sensitive to negative appraisals of his work. He regarded his age as an "impossible hurdle" for reentry into the job market. He discounted the encouragement of friends and colleagues as "temporary and well-meaning" and expected that he would have to "face the dragons" alone now. He procrastinated over many of the steps he needed to take for reemployment. He dawdled over the preparation of a resume; he postponed interviews. Despite a generous settlement that would allow for a substantial period without salary, he expected to be penniless and unemployed. He appraised himself as a "loser." He emphasized the stigma associated with being out of work. He saw himself as a failure.

The "empty nest syndrome" has been written about in detail. A woman in her late fifties came to see me just after she drove the youngest of her four children to college in North Carolina. She had dreaded this occasion "for years," as she wasn't sure the relationship with her husband "provided any real nourishment for her." Out of the job market for 30 years, she felt "hopelessly underskilled to function as a nurse" and unable, at her age, to start anew in another field. Her interests centered around her home and her children. Her husband defined himself largely by means of his occupation, from which she felt quite excluded. Facing the future, she felt sad, alone, and overwhelmed.

COGNITIVE WORK

Short-term treatment for problems with separation focuses first on the *personal meaning* of the situation encountered, whether marriage, job, or child-related. Then, *options* are generated by collaborative dialogue, polling relevant others, and supplementary reading. Options are defined as "choices," with the lever for self-control located within the patient's grasp. When self-worth is eroded by fallout from the interpretation of the event, lengthier psychotherapy is generally prescribed. When symptoms of depression include sleep and appetite disorders and weight loss, as well as loss of energy, constant fatigue, and loss of usual pleasures and interests, an antidepressant drug is often prescribed to complement the psychotherapy. When anxiety generated in reaction to the assigned meanings of the situation impairs functioning, a trial of a minor tranquilizer may supplement cognitive therapy.

There is some immediate gain in sharing with a therapist one's reaction to a marital separation. Conveying to the patient that you have treated this problem before diminishes (somewhat) the sense of aloneness that is experienced. A separated woman in her midforties presented for psychotherapy saying, "We have been apart for two years, yet I still feel addicted to him. I have not lost the image of what I thought he was, although I know it's not real." She had steadfastly opposed his attempts to reconcile; however, she maintained that she continued to feel "horribly rejected by him." The legal aspects of their separation were mired in a lengthy court battle, prolonging the process of detachment from him.

The analogy of a relationship to a drug implied by the concept of "addiction" is commonly encountered. The icon discussed in the last chapter is equally relevant here as a mechanism for dealing with separation. The need to achieve a realistic view of an ex-spouse is paramount before one can begin the work of retooling one's own self-image. Arrangements made for custody and visitation of children or legal disputes about division of property or finances frequently complicate the patient's attempt to let go of the relationship and move on.

With my separating patient, we formed a problem list:

1. Detach from spouse.
2. Change your mode of relating to him.
3. Deal with the icon.
4. Develop a court strategy.
5. Learn to like yourself enough to not *need* someone else.

For each issue, relevant cognitions were identified and tested. She was encouraged to challenge some. I actively confronted others. For example, she thought of the court battle as an all-or-nothing fight "for her life." Worse, she was convinced that her powerful husband could not lose it. The intensity of her sense of rejection was seen as related to the image that had persisted of her spouse as kind, gentle, and caring. As her view of him became more realistic, the impact of being rejected lessened.

The final (self-image) issue took the most work and ranged across considerations of her new career and her skill as a parent, as well as the feedback she received from new friends she had met. These appraisals were juxtaposed with her self-attitudes, reinforced by her husband's statements and actions over their 20-year marriage. She was encouraged to *update* her self-view to account for the "newer" data.

Another woman had been separated for almost four years when she presented for psychotherapy. She was managing a career along with three small children when she became aware of persistent anxiety and depression. Consistent cognitive errors of polarization, personalization, and overgeneralization dominated her thinking. A tendency to infer rejection quickly in relationships with men had brought her a great deal of emotional pain. Her conclusions, "I am destined to be alone. Being alone means I have failed. If I am not loved, I have no value. I need other people. To tell a man how I feel is to drive him away," were defined as maintaining her anxiety and depression.

After five sessions in which I helped her identify, challenge, and reframe her thinking about various significant relationships, she reported "feeling good for the first time in years. I am thinking slightly differently about things." Over the next five sessions, her view of herself as a victim emerged as a prominent theme. Once again, cognitions relevant to specific situations were identified, errors were noted, and alternatives were discussed. She felt she was now "spending less time occupied with her own misery."

Toward therapy's termination, sessions were dominated by developing a willingness to take reasonable social risks—to "allow herself to be vulnerable again." Meanwhile, she had left a job that demanded little of her (and returned little to her) for one that "acknowledged her strengths and surrounded her with decent people." Since the job provided tuition benefits, she was encouraged to return to the pursuit of a desired career, earlier abandoned.

In all, the psychotherapy lasted nine months. It initially considered her thinking about men and relationships. Then it focused on her relationship with her husband. Finally it centered upon her view of herself, her own potential, and ways of realizing it.

Some people seek therapeutic help when their sense of self has become dependent upon another in several key areas of functioning, and then separation occurs. Others consult a therapist when a spouse has assumed a representation in their life that can't be easily replaced, and then separation occurs. Less frequently, the person perpetrating the separation cannot deal alone with its consequences for his or her spouse. This was the situation when a man in his early thirties called me after he had decided to leave his wife of 10 years. She had not accepted his leaving, and his responses to her varied from support and caring (seen by her as indicators of imminent reconciliation) to repeated statements of his unwavering plan to separate (seen by her as rejection and cruelty). His thinking was organized around a sense of his responsibility for her reactions. He had made little attempt to focus on life as a single person and to adapt to his new surroundings. He was withdrawn, depressed, and afraid when the phone rang that it would bring awful news from or about his wife.

Encouraged to focus more on *his* adaptation, he gradually established a place for himself in his new community. This place combined his work, his preferred form of recreation, and the shaping of an apartment to reflect his tastes and pleasures. He began to meet people, both men and women, and defined some "avoidant" behaviors, which he was able to change. He then focused on the legal requirements necessary for a separation agreement. He became more aware of "who he was," separate from who he and his ex-wife had become as a couple. As his perspective shifted from short-term to longitudinal, he began to like himself more and to rediscover his spirit of adventure.

There were 20 psychotherapy sessions over an eight-month period, with one year of follow-up sessions. Initially, therapy was devoted to defining which tasks of separation logically were his and which belonged to his spouse. He could not provide a new life for her, although he had often functioned in the role of "responsible party" in their marriage. Her misinterpretation of support as an interest to reconcile put him in a "no win" situation. His focus on her needs had eroded his time and enthusiasm for making his own transition to a single life. Once he had worked out the issue of responsibility, he began to accept his wife's choices as "her own." Then he was able to confront the identity issues of who he wanted to be and what he wanted to do. He demonstrated competence in applying the cognitive method on his own to a series of interim situations that had arisen. A follow-up letter many years later conveyed the many gains he attributed to his time in therapy. This man was one of those patients who worked well in therapy, but accomplished more on his own once regular sessions had ended by applying what he had learned.

In late twentieth-century America, the concept of a person's being "married to his or her job" is well established. Some spend a large share of each 24-hour day at work, six or seven days a week. For this subgroup, the "self-esteem pie" usually has a large slice representing work achievement. Success in relationships, parenting, or a leisure-time hobby may not be able to overcome a perceived failure on the job. The office "culture" may demand or reinforce this over-allocation of time to work. I remember being most unpopular in my residency program when I told the chief that having a new baby daughter would preclude my joining him on Saturday for an optional discussion of interesting clinical problems. I felt that she would only be an infant for a short while and I wasn't going to miss out on this stage of her life to demonstrate my enthusiasm for work. Surely, I could demonstrate this in some other way.

Typical of the "separated from job" presentations is a man in mid-life who consulted me because he was aware that he was being systematically excluded from the lines of decision at a job he had held for many years. For the previous five years he had suffered with the consequences. To explain his endurance, he cited his passivity and a fear of unemployment. He had developed signs of depression and had begun to withdraw from family responsibilities. In an initial session, he spoke with feeling about his need to leave the job. Although they were allowing him to "twist in the wind," he felt incapable of taking any action. He expressed his anger at the leadership of his firm for its failure to utilize what he did well and for discriminatory treatment of a "veteran worker." He had received an evaluation that he considered biased and inaccurate. An initial homework assignment involved reviewing the appraisal, identifying its conclusions, and listing data that confirmed or refuted the statements made.

He appeared for the next session without having done the homework. I decided against framing this as a noncompliance issue or a sign of his passivity. Instead, we did the homework together in the office. Subsequently, he took the first positive step toward leaving, exploring with relevant sources the range of options for a settlement agreement, should he leave. His cognitions (e.g.,"No one will hire me") were identified, and he was challenged to support or abandon them. His self-appraisal as a "loser" was reframed by him into one who had "done a good job under exceedingly difficult circumstances." He cited a collection of positive assessments he had been given by the many colleagues who had worked with him over his lengthy career.

We discussed his view of the future with regard to its uncertainties, his sense of insecurity and the need for appropriate risk-

taking. By the seventh session he had left work and h[ ]
job search with reasonable optimism. He saw himsel[ ]
able" and was beginning to consider situations suitabl[ ]
employment. He took pride in his assertive leave-taking, especially
as he looked back on the lengthy period of distress when he was
unable to act.

He began actively to process the positive feedback he had received and to consider some reasons that were neither personal nor specific to him for his mistreatment at the hands of newer and younger leadership. He considered this interim time as one of some advantages, as opposed to a period of pure peril. He spent more time with his wife, and it was a happy time. He attended daytime events at his children's school, an option he normally saw as closed to him. We spaced our sessions now to once monthly.

By the eleventh meeting (over a six-month period), he was satisfied that he had found a suitable job, had grown in the process of leaving, and had made good use of a short-term cognitive psychotherapy.

8

Older People Never Change

It is hard to argue with the premise that much of an individual's behavior, emotion, and thought is influenced by learning. Some of this learning takes place in the earliest years through a combination of role modeling, feedback, cultural factors, and experience. One's repertoire is enlarged in the negotiation of the various life stages of childhood, adolescence, and adulthood.

It is only logical that "habits," whether they be behaviors, emotional reactions, or cognitive patterns, become more ingrained as they are repeated over time. With repetition, the individual becomes defined, to a degree, by his or her characteristic pattern of behaving, reacting, and thinking. The longer this process goes on, the more "set in his way" an individual can be expected to become. One consequence of this prevalent process is that we often view older persons as rigid, habituated, and unlikely to change.

Consequently, older people have been seen as poor candidates for psychotherapy, even though they may possess many of the characteristics that make change likely. They may be greatly distressed, highly motivated to work hard, and blessed with the psychological mindedness that usually predicts a successful outcome. But, by subscribing to the cultural meaning given to chronological age, we cancel out their advantageous traits. The chapter title is meant to capture this societal belief; it is not to be taken literally.

As a new psychotherapist, I eagerly sought patients who were young, verbal and well-educated. When I was referred an older person, I assumed that the psychotherapeutic work would involve identifying the patient's strengths and "supporting" them, rather than encouraging new learning.

My attitude changed about eight years ago when I met a 65–year–old man, self-referred for cognitive therapy. He had read about it in *Life* magazine. One exchange in our opening session went like this:

A.R.: I have been depressed for most of my life — this despite a satisfactory work life as the head of my own insurance firm. I have had two courses of psychoanalytic therapy — 10 years of each. I believe I know most of what I can learn about depression.

D.S.: All right, then, I'll bite. If you've learned most of what there is to know about depression, what brings you to see me?

A.R.: After 20 years of psychoanalysis, I'm just as depressed now as I was then. I am hoping that a different approach might enable me to feel better.

I was skeptical about what he could accomplish in a cognitive mode after 20 years of psychotherapy had brought little change. But A.R. was a thoughtful, intelligent, introspective man, with a delightful sense of humor that emerged as his depression cleared. He worked hard, sustained a high level of motivation, and seemed to prepare specifically for each session.

When I met A.R., he was married, a father and grandfather, and he had multiple, but not disabling, medical problems: peptic ulcer, arthritis, and a substantial hearing deficit. Diagnostically, he met DSM-III[34] criteria for dysthymic disorder (earlier, chronic characterological depression).

A.R. was abandoned by his father at an early age; then his mother was hospitalized for a chronic illness during his early adolescence and died in the hospital. This led to a period of time living with relatives, in foster homes, and finally with cousins while he attended college. He had met his wife-to-be while a teenager and after college graduation they married. They had several children, and he started his business.

In our early sessions, we identified eight basic schemas relevant to his depression:

1. He constantly expected abandonment and rejection.
2. He constantly expected to be cheated or frustrated, especially if he was not in complete control.
3. He had developed a need to be "seen and not heard" to avoid others' disapproval.
4. He expected his firm to lose its clients and go bankrupt.

5. He had minimal trust of others, including his wife of 40 years.
6. He was reluctant to spend money, believing that any "loss" of money meant an increase in vulnerability.
7. He described his persistent pessimism as "always looking for the mold in the bread."
8. He continually expected to be punished for unspecified misdeeds.

These basic beliefs led to a persistent sad mood, an unwillingness to risk, multiple avoidance behaviors, and little perception of choice.

In once weekly cognitive therapy, he has learned:

1. To use mood shifts and feelings of anxiety and sadness as cues to do cognitive work: identifying automatic thoughts associated with his basic underlying beliefs, challenging them, and generating alternatives.
2. To pay more attention to current feedback ("update the résumé") and to challenge attitudes rooted in the past.
3. To take reasonable risks.
4. To relax; to enjoy sex.
5. To see choices more often; to generate options.
6. To develop a trusting relationship with his wife.
7. To be comfortable when alone.
8. To be comfortable attending parties, even with people he is meeting for the first time.
9. To "discount" less often.
10. To like himself more. (This has led to an easier time spending money on himself.)
11. To use a fine sense of humor effectively. (He once told me, "I'm so private a person, I even keep things from myself.")
12. To maintain his new weight, achieved via a 30–pound weight loss, and initiate an exercise regimen to keep in shape.

The usual qualifiers apply. There was no control group, so attributing changes to therapy is an hypothesis. Some other approach might have worked as well (however, his long exposure to apparently "good" analytic therapy with minimal change belies this). The relationship factors were not insignificant. I have a great deal of love and respect for him.

My experience with A.R. has led to more psychotherapeutic work with older people and less hesitance to contract for long-term work (see Chapter 9). In brief cognitive therapy, I have found that some older depressed and anxious patients are as motivated for change as their younger counterparts. They identify specific agendas and work with me in a way indistinguishable from that used by my younger patients. Many, having had prior experience with non-directive psychotherapy, find the cognitive dialogue stimulating and "a welcome change." The cognitive model is easy to learn. With some older patients, I find myself utilizing more structure (blackboard, triple column, specific homework assignments); however, with others a cognitive *framework* seems to suffice. Again, this is no different from the treatment of younger persons.

Here is a typical referral. A woman in her early seventies was referred to me by her family doctor. Her husband (of 50 years) had sustained a disabling illness almost two years earlier. She was now suffering fairly constant anxiety, concerned that he would (for example) set a fire while smoking, fall due to his impaired vision, or fail due to unaccustomed memory problems. She missed the bright, attentive, stimulating partner she had known. She saw herself as a "screaming witch." Her husband needed help to dress himself, could no longer read, and had a poor sense of balance. She could not predict when he would be "able" and when he would be impaired.

She described to me their life together, their children, and his work as well as her own. There were many sources of contentment. "Mainly," she said, "I feel trapped by the way his illness has changed our lives."

Cognitive principles were presented to her in brief. Her over-concern with what others might think when they saw her husband was noted. Her error in "personalizing" his actions, inferring that they were somehow "meant for her," was discussed. The withdrawal of her friends was seen as a logical consequence of *her* reaction to her husband's disability. Initiative on her part could result in reconnection with her social network. The need to accept the changes in her spouse without overgeneralizing, as well as the concurrent need to pursue the stimulation she required alone, was discussed with her.

In the third and fourth sessions, she reported feeling a lot better. She told me that she had "more perspective and more awareness of what I do to limit myself." She was now more willing to compromise, while asserting herself to have more of her needs met. We parted after this brief time together, after I expressed my availability to her for further sessions at her initiative.

Some themes are more common to the life experience of an older person than to that of someone younger. With aging, physical illness more often intrudes into daily life. The phenomenon of losing significant others to death is more frequent. Some capacities central to maintaining control over the environment may diminish, with anxiety and depression accompanying an awareness of one's vulnerability. The "culture" treats an older person differently, often assigning expectations and restrictions based upon chronological age rather than capability. One's place in the family may change. Mandatory retirement may separate an older person from a key aspect of his or her identity. An awareness of not having reached a life goal may become a central concern, if the individual believes that the goal is no longer within reach.

As I began to treat older persons more frequently, I grew to expect these themes. Periodically, I was "surprised" to hear about a problem that had little connection to the age of the person. Such was the case when a man in his early eighties was referred by his internist because of a conflict he was having with his brother. He described his (younger) brother as rigid, authoritarian, and demanding. His response to a confrontation was always to back down, with the result that he felt "lousy," couldn't sleep, and became preoccupied with the issue. He described his life path in brief, with emphasis on the development of his relationship with his brother. He believed that expressing himself would result in his brother's getting angry, and he didn't want that to happen. He told of a similar series of interactions he had with a neighbor. She had taken advantage of him and he could not tell her so. He had spent days brooding about this as well.

He was instructed in the cognitive model, with blackboard illustration of situations, feelings, and automatic thoughts. The cognitive error of personalization and the technique of decentering were each discussed with him. We generated several different options for dealing with anger. The cognitive error of catastrophizing was described, and he laughed at an elaborate analogy relevant to someone else's life. He immediately focused on the link to his problem and talked in detail about his plan to speak with his brother.

Over the next two sessions, he described conversations he had with his brother (and his neighbor) on several occasions. He reported feeling relieved and was pleasantly surprised by each of their reactions. After four weeks, he said that he had "learned his lesson" and "would not be bashful to call again, if necessary."

Of a man in his sixties, I once asked, "Given your age, what explains how hard you have been working to change? How many years of life could you have to enjoy the relief or benefits of feeling better?" Mr. P. indignantly replied, "No one knows how long they're going to live—not even you. You might be hit by a car and killed in your own parking lot. I've felt depressed for more than 50 years. However many years are left to me, I'd rather feel good than continue on as I have been." I felt no need to ever inquire about this again!

This patient was given my name by a longtime friend. He had worked for many years in psychotherapy to combat chronic symptoms of depression and anxiety. He had tried several new forms of treatment, as well as years of group therapy. He had tried on his own to gain understanding that might affect his mood state as well. As a last resort, he agreed to consult a cognitive therapist.

His life had been an interesting one, with travel far and wide and multiple involvements in helping less fortunate others. Mr. P. related poorly to authority figures (frequently seeing them as "enemies"). He was a perfectionist by nature who rarely reached his own elevated standards. He easily lost perspective in situations, retreating to concrete (literal) positions that told others he "didn't understand them" and that he "took himself too seriously." He suffered from social anxiety and would deliberately place himself on the periphery of office groups. He constantly anticipated rejection. He spoke in a rambling, discursive fashion. I wondered initially about organic mental changes, but more contact revealed a man who could focus, concentrate, retain, and recall. The working diagnosis was chronic depression.

This bright and thoughtful man was concerned about what would be the legacy of his time on earth. He felt he had not distinguished himself in his chosen field. His marriage had not worked out well. His children had confronted several serious life problems. He had few friends. It was hard for him to accept responsibility, especially in the context of a relationship. He felt that he was overly concerned with the approval of others.

We worked on establishing a reasonable self-appraisal. After about 20 sessions, he reported some "good days" when things were "clearer" and that he was less mired in detail. He was less afraid, others noticed a "glow" in him, and he felt that a "process" had begun. We had developed an easy, nonthreatening, often joking rapport. Our work together was clearly going to take a longer time than the traditional cognitive therapy model I was used to. Neither Mr. P nor I felt constrained by expectations of rapid change.

He talked about his chronic difficulty dealing with the "emotions of love." There were real ambiguities in his sense of identity. It was hard for him to surrender control. As his time in therapy neared one year, there were further gains. Clearly feeling better about himself, he began taking some social initiative. Other people were "becoming more real" to him. He was beginning to evolve a definition of who he was and to set some priorities for his life. He met a woman who was attractive to him.

A particularly difficult issue arose when he saw his son "developing, in some ways, just like me" and felt powerless to help. A second crisis came when his new female friend ended their relationship. His initial reaction was to blame himself on both accounts. Decentering helped him to regain perspective. An earlier problem with confrontation became relevant again. Each time, we stressed the meanings he found in events and situations, identified cognitive errors (chiefly personalization and polarization), and proposed alternative strategies. He became aware that he had established his friend as the repository of his newfound self–worth. When she left him, he felt that much of his gain had left with her.

His response was to return to the notion of legacy and the building of a dream. It was here that my ill-conceived remark was made about his age and prospects. Our relationship survived even this extreme instance of insensitivity. He moved successfully to a new home. He had always defined himself in terms of the needs of others. That would now change.

At the two–year mark, we assessed progress. He felt "more flexible" in his thinking. He more often "felt normal." However, he continued to feel "vulnerable to depressed moods and pessimistic modes of thinking" in times of crisis. Over the holiday period, he demonstrated to himself some of his newly acquired social skills. He was taking things "less seriously" and functioning far better at work.

After three years of once weekly therapy, he reported "liking himself more" and experiencing feelings that had been "absent" during most of his life. We began discussing risk-taking and the concept of choice in great detail. He reported feeling "relaxed" for the first time "in years." We had already begun spacing visits every two, then every three weeks. He commented that the depression "had attenuated." He was making decisions now, more definitely and more quickly.

He had a brief depressive reaction to a job transfer, but regained perspective quickly. He felt he could now "evaluate people" better. He was able to "look people in the eye." He could see things, at times, from the other person's vantage point. He was less interpersonally domineering, more willing to listen.

Cognitive therapy lasted for more than four years, with sessions held monthly for the final 15 months. There appeared to be demonstrable characterological changes. He was now rarely depressed and generally interpersonally involved and skilled, with a clearer self-definition and some optimism for the future.

His age proved to be no obstacle to achieving change. The characterological elements required lengthy repetition and continued confrontation before they succumbed. However, Mr. P. was a worthwhile investment of therapeutic time and effort.

It is clear to me that older people do indeed change. Little distinguishes this group from the younger cohort, except that issues of changing self-definition, retirement, and the death of significant others occur with increased frequency. As a group, older people are no more or less motivated, no more or less hardworking, no more or less creative or clever. Thanks to a societal expectation of less likelihood of achieving change, they are (if anything) more appreciative of the opportunity to experience change in psychotherapy.

IV

Extending the Model

9
Long-Term
Cognitive Therapy

F_{or} years, I was skeptical that long-term therapy worked for anyone, whether patient or therapist. I attributed success, when it occurred, to a high level of personal motivation in the patient, combined with the benefits of the nonspecific (relationship) aspects of the psychotherapy transaction. Yet it was claimed that intensive psychoanalytic psychotherapy helped people make changes in "character" or "personality." The dictionary definition of personality is, "the organization of the individual's distinguishing character traits, attitudes or habits . . . the totality of an individual's behavioral and emotional tendencies." It is noteworthy that the definition does not specify (for example) "a set of dynamics based upon the impact of unconscious conflicts, best understood considering the interplay of forces of id, ego and superego, and best approached by an introspective review of early childhood development." Nevertheless, most clinicians seem to accept that personality change can be achieved only through psychoanalytic methods aimed at achieving insight into unconscious processes. I know of no evidence attesting to the accuracy of this judgment.

I asked myself, if the model is a vehicle that provides the language in which the person and problems are conceptualized, what benefit does a psychodynamic language have over a cognitive language? I could see none. The psychoanalytic approach to change appeared to me to present its active process ingredients in a rather obscure and inefficient fashion. The cognitive model appeared to approach reframing quite directly and to avoid the necessity of spending undue time in a study of the patient's past. Finally, if basic rules (or schemas) could actually be changed over time, it seemed logical that affect and behavior would change to be consistent with them.

How, then, could the short-term model that involved identifying automatic thoughts and cognitive errors and then generating and testing alternatives be adapted to facilitate "personality change"? The obvious candidate for a cognitive focus would be the basic rules or principles (schemas) that governed the individual's thinking. These schemas are the building blocks of a person's thinking and give rise to the moment–to–moment beliefs Beck has called automatic thoughts.

In a short-term model, the relevant schemas were not usually hard to identify. In a long-term approach, these rules would be the focus of the psychotherapy. What would it take to effect the "character change" that long-term psychoanalytic therapy claims as its target? Would higher order cognitive change suffice?

I accepted a few patients with the stated goal of "character change." I expected the work to be longer, harder, and more repetitious than its brief counterpart. It made intuitive sense that schemas, like habits practiced over many years, would be resistant to change. Dislodging a central or defining belief would leave the patient feeling vulnerable and dependent upon the relationship with the therapist.

PRINCIPLES OF LONG-TERM COGNITIVE THERAPY

Over the past eight years, I have treated an increasing number of patients utilizing a modification of the cognitive model as a framework for long-term psychotherapy. Sessions are usually limited to once weekly. Duration of therapy is measured in years, rather than in weeks. Several patients have achieved major gains. Several principles have evolved to guide this long-term work. While the therapist-patient relationship seems important in brief therapy, its significance increases as the time spent together lengthens. Therefore, special attention must be paid to harnessing the *nonspecific aspects* (see Chapter 1) of successful psychotherapy. Engagement is highlighted, including the match between therapist and patient, and a clear statement of goals, roles, and expectations is made at the outset. When the match is a poor one, referral is encouraged.

Central to the therapeutic work is the *identification of schemas*. Initially, a collection of automatic thoughts is made in a variety of situations, with an eye toward spotting the basic rule from which the cognitions derive. Once a schema is found, the range of automatic thoughts to which it gives rise is noted. When several schemas can be agreed upon with some certainty, a cognitive definition of the individual may be specified. Emotional reactions and typical behaviors in certain situations define patterns that form an outline of the patient's cognitive structure. Usually, it is not difficult for the patient to locate the schemas he or she believes to be responsible for distress.

At some point, I acknowledge to the patient that a person's *basic rules may have been adaptive in earlier life circumstances*. The operative questions are: Are they adaptive now or have they been retained, unquestioned, out of habit? Do they take into account what the patient has learned *since* childhood? Has the resumé been updated?

Once a schema has been chosen as a focus, an experiment may be proposed to test its validity or to generate alternate strategies. Input may come from the patient's reading, his or her awareness of another's approach to the same situation, or the advice of a friend or significant other. The tedious part involves constant observation and testing of both the schema and the proposed alternatives, over a wide range of situations. Often, a log is kept and discussed at each session. Its format is yet another modification of the triple column, now consisting of: situations, feelings, automatic thoughts, schema, and alternative rule. With situation piling atop situation, and time passing in the process, change (when it occurs) is usually gradual. There is frequent backsliding and return of "old thinking." At these times, the support and encouragement of a committed therapist are crucial. Often the process is facilitated by engaging a significant other to rally some support among the patient's other close relations.

Frequently, the patient and I examine together the *meaning of risk* in a variety of contexts. At times, the nature of the risk is quantified and a graded schedule of risk-taking is established. Cognitions generated in anticipation of risk, as well as during performance, are studied in detail. One desired endpoint is a change in the patient's willingness to take risks. Another is the establishment of a rational process of risk assessment that leads to a balance between assertion and caution acceptable to the patient.

I work extensively with long–term patients on the concept of *choice* and on evaluating the consequences of various choices. Attributions for actions or beliefs are too frequently assigned to external events, to the patient's view of "consensus," or to a sense of moral obligation. Examples of *external attributions* are: "Because my father was an alcoholic, I am often depressed." "Because the teacher doesn't teach, I failed the course." "Because of my handicap, I couldn't accomplish the task." While the response to an overwhelming event may be uniform, most situations permit a wide range of interpretations.

I have learned to be wary of statements that begin with: "Everyone knows that . . . " or "All other women have . . . " or "No one I know would even consider. . . . " Clearly, *comparison with others* is one guideline we use to establish the boundaries around some of our choices. This policy is abused, however, when it is used to squelch creativity or force conformity to a perceived norm.

Ellis[20] has elaborated the idea that people often make attributions to their sense of *what should be done*. I often ask my patients: "Who is the authority, to which the 'should' can be traced? Is it possible to evaluate the 'should statement' much as one would any other choice? Or must it be followed blindly to avoid the guilt attendant upon questioning it?" These discussions may range into a review of a patient's religious beliefs, cultural expectations, or parental proscriptions. I stress *not* rejecting these ideas, but rather subjecting them to the same appraisal given other alternatives.

Whatever the personality style of the long-term patient, I have found that psychotherapy frequently considers the generic issues of *expressivity, independence, and assertiveness*, within the context of choosing adaptive interpersonal strategies. Many with an obsessive-compulsive style are aware of feelings they have, but sharing them with others has not been a frequent choice for them. The advantages and disadvantages of this approach are considered. Clues to recognizing "hidden" feelings are discussed.

For the hitherto dependent individual, the traits necessary to overcome reliance on others are pointed out. Experiments may be proposed to try out action options that would permit an individual to function more independently. The benefits of dependency (in some situations), as well as the concept that most of us rely upon others some of the time, are brought into the transaction at some point.

For the more passive individual, psychotherapy incorporates the teaching of assertiveness. This often dovetails with the segment on risk assessment. The goal is to teach and model behaviors that allow the patient to advocate for him or herself in a variety of situations. As with dependency, the virtues of at times listening and waiting, as opposed to taking action, are stressed. An attempt is made to encourage a spectrum of responses, with assertion at one end and passivity at the other.

When an ongoing style or a chronic problem is the focus of the treatment, special attention must be paid to the *arrangement of mastery experiences*. Whether through experiments designed to teach mastery or via taking advantage of natural life opportunities, one can pursue opportunities to succeed, which can be powerfully reinforcing in their own right. Success may lead to a willingness to take further risks and pave the way for more success.

When change occurs in schemas, an early and sensitive indicator is often a *change in automatic thoughts*. Most patients are sensitive to this, reporting, "I approached the same situation I've encountered before, but in a different way this time. When I compared my log with an earlier one, it was evident that my 'reflex thoughts' were not the same as before." These changes often correlate with a decrease in anxiety and depression, as reported by the patient.

To illustrate the principles of long-term cognitive therapy, let me introduce you to Mrs. T. When she came to therapy, she was 50 years old and had been married (for the second time) for seven years. Her problems with alcohol could be traced to her move to Washington from the midwest eight years earlier. She was guilty about leaving her elderly father and somewhat relieved when he died two years after she came east. Meanwhile, she met and married her second husband, amid great expectations. She gained nearly 60 pounds (to a weight of 200 lbs.) over a period of five years. Her husband apparently spent long hours at work and little time at home. She felt that in the past year he had withdrawn from her, and their sexual relationship had stopped. On several occasions, he told her that he didn't love her anymore.

Mrs. T. tended to internalize feelings and build anger which she didn't express openly. She was extremely sensitive to what others said and did, frequently personalizing others' actions. She believed that she was difficult to get along with. She suspected that her alcohol habit, although she hid it, might be a disruptive factor in her marriage.

She had held a responsible corporate job until she left the midwest. During her second marriage she had not worked. Mrs. T. maintained a close relationship with an internist and used some of their time together to discuss her concerns. The internist was skeptical about the usefulness of her consulting a psychiatrist.

Over the six months prior to her consultation with me, she became progressively depressed. She overate, drank to excess, and had a hard time falling back to sleep after waking up in the middle of the night. She withdrew from friends and activity. She continued to gain weight, had a negative view of herself, and became quite pessimistic about the future. She blamed herself for the deterioration of her marriage and felt helpless to do anything about it.

Her father was a corporate executive who died of heart disease. Her mother had died earlier of cancer. She had a sister several years older who managed a store in Texas. There was no family history of emotional illness.

Mrs. T. had been graduated from Ohio State University with a degree in economics. She interrupted her college education to work and put her first husband through school. He got a good job, but his first company went bankrupt. She worked for a corporation, doing accounting for almost 12 years. She saw the downhill course of her first marriage as "strikingly similar" to what she was going through with Mr. T. today.

My initial impressions included: (1) major depressive disorder, as well as dysthymic disorder; (2) alcoholism; (3) exogenous obesity; (4) marital discord. An antidepressant drug trial seemed indicated. I received her permission to talk with her internist. Mrs. T. and I formed a contract for cognitive therapy. I agreed to see her husband collaterally and perhaps to do couples therapy, if it seemed warranted. Her priorities were: (1) her marriage; (2) her depression; (3) her alcoholism; (4) her weight gain.

A low dose of an antidepressant drug brought immediate side effects and was discontinued. Further chemotherapy was tabled for the moment. In the initial discussions, the problem focus was her marriage. She felt that her husband's work, not the relationship, was his first priority. She felt "trapped" in the relationship, as she depended upon her husband but had "little life" with him. She felt that her needs were ignored. Her husband was initially unwilling to come in for an evaluative visit with me. She blamed herself for the lack of success in her marriage, validating her low self-worth. In addition, she avoided confrontations, seeking to please Mr. T., while her anger at the course of events continued to build.

After five sessions, Mr. T. came to my office. He told me that he saw his wife and himself as "different types." He stressed his commitment to the marriage and his willingness to attend joint sessions if that might help. He indicated that he no longer felt "any real love" for his wife. He liked being alone.

Five joint sessions followed. I explored with each of them how they assigned meanings to the behavior of the other. They each saw their styles as "incompatible." She was overly sensitive. He was passive, would not initiate or take risks. She felt continually taken advantage of. She expected him to "figure out what she needed him to do."

During this time, an issue emerged that engaged their commitment to work together. His daughter (by a previous marriage) had a problem requiring their help. Seeing Mr. T.'s initially negative response, Mrs. T. felt comfortable for the first time discussing with him their marital incompatibility. This discussion led to Mr. T.'s confronting the possibility of the end of his marriage. His behavior changed suddenly and markedly toward his wife. Mrs. T., meanwhile, was assertive and sensitive in her response to her stepdaughter. This sequence drew the couple closer and cooled the separation issue for the moment.

Since Mrs. T. needed to do considerable work, individual sessions with her were resumed. We focused on her self-worth and how she processed data, her expressivity and what she expected from others. She no longer felt that her marriage was "necessary" for her to feel good. Over the next few weeks, she noticed that her husband was staying late at work. She considered several meanings: rejection of her? another woman? workaholism? She began a diet and found a weight loss program to which she considered making a commitment.

She defined her problem with self-assertion as one of polarized thinking. She could be a "bitch" or a "pushover." We identified some midground alternatives. Unfortunately, there seemed to be no grays regarding her marriage. She consulted an attorney and began again to consider separation. She noted that, when depression enveloped her (Mrs. T.'s concept), she blamed herself exclusively for "two failed marriages." She felt that she was finally confronting her marital problem honestly, and some sadness followed. Now she started to focus on her alcoholism and reviewed her substance abuse history with me in detail. She also began attending Alcoholics Anonymous meetings.

Six months after therapy began, Mr. and Mrs. T. had agreed to separate. She had lost 15 pounds in anticipation of beginning the diet program. Her alcohol habit was coming under control, and she regularly attended AA.

In the next six weeks she lost twenty-five pounds, made a number of good friends in the program and continued to reformulate her self–view. She began to focus in therapy on Mr. T.'s passivity regarding carrying out the separation, and developed several possible explanations:

1. There was still a chance for their marriage.
2. He was proceeding "by his own timetable."
3. He was concerned about her ability to "survive without him."

We discussed these alternatives and she accepted the notion that Mr. T. was probably doing what was best for him.

Mrs. T. began to "update her cognitive résumé" by searching for a job that would provide an important building block in reworking her life. She was riddled with self–doubt. We now concentrated for several months on her view of herself as a worker. She feared failure and had little self-confidence. She had been "out of the market" for too long. She acknowledged that she felt "as good as she had seven years ago," save for continuing to blame herself for the "marriage failure." She saw a future of "interpersonal aloneness." By now, she had lost 60 pounds and was becoming quite satisfied with how she looked at age 51.

There were several "dates" with Mr. T., each ending with a depressed mood and a view of herself as "defective." She believed that she was a "poor judge of men" and would "always be alone." The errors of selective abstraction and arbitrary inference were frequent in her self-assessment after she spent time with Mr. T. She identified the "finality of her separation" from Mr. T. as the factor undermining her self–worth. She had assigned too large a slice of her self–esteem pie to the status of "being married."

We discussed the uncontrollability of outcomes. She described a sense of perfectionism that lay at the root of her "return to work" fears. She had now been in therapy for one year and abstinent from alcohol for six months. She thought that she had achieved a more rational view of Mr. T. and of herself over the past six months of therapy. Mostly, she now liked what she saw in herself, except for the schema of self-blame still attached to her marriage. She believed that "depression and alcoholism permitted her to remain in a relationship that was bad for her." Was she avoiding the stress and challenge of once again being single? Mr. T.'s lack of sensitivity, his passivity, and his incapacity for intimacy made him a poor choice for a mate. Her error, therefore, was in *choosing* him, not in failing to make the marriage work. "You can, with difficulty, make changes in yourself," she said, "but you can't change someone else."

She was pleased that she had been able to lose weight and then stay at an acceptable level. She was proud of "no longer being involved with alcohol," but believed that she would have to maintain her vigilance to maintain sobriety. She planned to continue frequent attendance at AA meetings. Two big issues were conquered, and two remained. Her self-view was not yet where it needed to be, and she remained apprehensive about her upcoming return to the work world.

We reviewed the predictors — pro and con — available from the past relevant to her current work performance. A balance sheet on the blackboard listed the positive and negative factors. As she went over them, we discussed what it would take to convince her of her "work worth." Only performance on the job would be persuasive to her. And that, she was aware, would be subject to the meanings she applied to events. Acute depression was no longer a problem; rather, the ongoing ways in which she made attributions seemed responsible for determining her mood over time.

Our sessions accompanied her through the interviews, the deliberations, and the final decision to accept a job offer. She identified automatic thoughts relevant to anticipatory anxiety that was her companion during her initial months at work.

I continued to see Mrs. T. weekly for three more months. Her initial adjustment at work was excellent, as she was extremely well received by coworkers and supervisors. She developed a small cadre of friends, largely through AA meeting attendance. We decided to shift into a follow-up phase of monthly visits and "await developments."

Over time, she received several work promotions. The first time she had to fire an employee was difficult for her, but sensitively managed. At the one-year anniversary of her sobriety, she gave a party and invited 20 guests.

When she was promoted to a position of "real responsibility," there was a brief "fear of failure." We discussed the need, once again, to update her (psychological) résumé regarding work performance and potential. The long period out of the work force had now been superseded by a one-year period of employment. The past year provided sufficient predictors of work success to counter her earlier anxieties.

Events like the Christmas holiday evoked a sense of aloneness, reawakening cognitions of relationship failure. We discussed her various social choices and some of their consequences. After one year of monthly visits, we began to meet quarterly. She signed a separation agreement. Her husband moved out of the area. She defined her goal now as a "search for a life structure." Much of her "self" was defined in terms of work, where rave reviews had resulted in leaps up the corporate ladder. Periodic personalization continued, but often she caught these now and developed alternative approaches.

We decreased visits to a frequency of once every six months. She was light years away from the depressed, overweight, alcoholic woman I had first encountered. She was aware of discomfort with intimacy and continued to shy away from taking social risks and initiative. Questioned about this, she maintained that she was not interested in exploring these areas further in psychotherapy.

Clearly, I had become a continuing figure in her life. Our contact, however, was now limited to "planned reviews" every six months. I rarely heard from her between follow-up visits. She was delighted by her success at work and change in personal habits. The impact of her marriage upon her sense of self–worth had diminished markedly with time. She continued to retool her self–view despite only infrequent therapeutic contact. Total time in psychotherapy was about one year, with five years of follow-up that continues, infrequently, to the present time.

10
Reparenting

The lay view of psychotherapy, especially of long-term psycho-therapy, is often that of one adult (the therapist) assigning blame for the problems of a child (the patient) to another set of adults (the parents). This "bashing of mom and dad" apparently shifts the responsibility for the patient's outcome from him or herself (often manifested as depression) to one or both parents (sometimes thought of as "healthy anger"). Allowing for a considerable degree of distortion (the therapist rarely interviews the parents at any length), a case is built to indict the parents in absentia.

A cognitive therapist would accomplish little with this ap-proach. It is central to the achievement of change, in my view, that the patient accept responsibility for his or her own thoughts, feelings, and behavior. We are each taught many things by our parents' example, their words to us, and their reactions to our behavior. Often our parents (and people in general) act in ways expected to gratify their own needs. Frequently, their actions re-sult from an active consideration of our best interests as children. Sometimes we must conclude that they do the best they can. Some-times other influences have formative effects on the development of the child.

In addition, the impact of parental teaching might not yet be obvious by the time of adolescence. What may be evident in the "child" is the lack of a structure on which to base the formation of an identity. Additionally, the child may be unable to achieve an effective separation from the parent(s). There may be inadequate self-definition to allow the pursuit of a career. Clinically, this pic-ture may produce depression and/or the characteristics subsumed in the amorphous label of borderline personality.

Most of my patients are in the age range of 30 to 50 years old. My growing interest in geriatrics accounts for a small "peak" at age 70. 1 accept few teenagers as patients, believing that adolescent "specialists" are better equipped to deal with this turbulent age group than I am. I have, however, treated a significant number of adolescents using a model I call *reparenting*. Typical of the younger person I have treated is a 17 to 27 year old, more often female than male, usually chronically depressed "kid," often in the midst of a crisis. He or she has "no one to turn to," despite having access to a "loving, interested parent (or parents)." There is usually a special reason for accepting the referral. Either it is the child of a person with whom I have some connection or an adolescent specifically referred for cognitive therapy who has had little benefit from other forms of psychotherapy.

A review of the past history reveals academic failure (typically in high school), relationship failure (poor choices and bad outcomes), and often some form of substance abuse. Typically, the adolescent has many friends (one of his or her strengths), is at least of average intelligence (another plus), has siblings and parents who have "achieved," and is not living up to anyone's expectations. The symptoms these adolescents present include depressed mood, pessimistic outlook and low self-esteem; generalized anxiety and often specific phobic avoidances, along with a variety of self-defeating behaviors.

Therapy is long-term (either continuous or intermittent for perhaps five years or longer). Despite the patient's having capable people as parents (who often have demonstrated effective parenting with other children), one framework for understanding these treatments is reparenting. I become accepted as an "alternative parent" and actively challenge the conceptual matrix the adolescent or young adult has formed to meet life's situations. Little by little on a succession of issues, old ideas are discussed, sometimes acted upon, reviewed, and labeled with regard to cognitive errors (where appropriate). Alternatives are sought, tried on and tried out. When the process works, change becomes evident to the patient, producing a certain momentum that facilitates further changes. For some life problems, the adolescent seems to have "no preparation" or an extremely inadequate (or bizarre) cognitive map. Often there is great inertia and fear of change, with withdrawal from, rather than confrontation of, a problem.

Identity formation seems always to be a therapeutic issue. Separation from family of origin is an issue as well. Low self–worth, within the context of passing school courses, finding a significant other, or furthering a career, is constantly encountered. In the borderline patients, there is often active antagonism toward the parents, and acting–out is associated with risk–taking behavior and often suicidal or homicidal acts. In the depressed adolescents, the clinical problem is more often avoidance and withdrawal than risk–taking behaviors.

An attempt is made to help the patient reformulate his or her self–view. In the process, the view of the parents is often reworked as well. This may enable the reestablishment of a supportive friendship in place of a combative clash that satisfied neither party.

The issues, while similar in content to those I encounter with adults, seem much more immediate, threatening, and central to the lives of these "teenagers" (whether the patient is in his or her teens or twenties, the problems dealt with are the typical adaptational events of adolescence). And always, there seems little "of substance" to fall back upon. Only after change and some achievement can the adolescent begin to rely on "recent success" to support optimism in the face of stress.

Let me paint a few life pictures to illustrate the range of presentations for which reparenting has seemed an appropriate description. A 26–year–old woman had endured several "near" marriages, one six–month marriage, and many unsatisfactory relationships of varying lengths. She had a strong need for approval, was highly dependent and rejection-sensitive, and frequently felt taken advantage of by men. When a relationship developed beyond the initial meetings, it invariably was labeled as a "last chance" for her.

In therapy, she began assembling the pieces of a functional identity. She defined career interests and put herself on a desired path. She established a framework for relating to her parents and became able to ignore some of their repetitive negative comments that used to prompt withdrawal. She became more willing to take social risks, and developed a more philosophical (and less catastrophizing) outlook on relationship outcomes.

Individual sessions often were oriented toward finding perspective on an ongoing situation. The result was that she frequently "felt good" after a therapy hour. When a goal was reached and therapy stopped, it often resumed around her reaction to a new stress: for example, illness in a family member or an unsatisfactory turn in a relationship.

Over a three–year period, she became noticeably more assertive, expressive, and self-confident and less demanding of others. She had "defined" a place for herself to be on a variety of life issues.

Another woman in her mid-twenties presented with a raft of anxiety symptoms, a tendency to ruminate, and dependency on, but alienation from, her family. She could not find a satisfactory job or form a satisfying relationship. She, too, was rejection-sensitive and, even more so, highly attuned to the approval of others.

She was phobic of driving, about being out after dark, and in general, about confronting novel places and situations. She continually made (negative) arbitrary inferences and overgeneralizations.

We worked at generating options, countering her negativity and identifying the ultimate consequences in many of her feared situations. She persevered through a series of unhappy job situations. She married a man who offered her some of what she wanted in life, while necessitating some real compromises by her as well. She achieved some acceptance of those traits in her parents that were unlikely ever to change. Meanwhile, she "became" an identifiable individual — far from a parental reprint — who exemplified some qualities of her mother and father but was specifically dissimilar in many important ways. Psychotherapy continued for five years.

A 22–year–old man was referred by a close friend of his when he expressed dissatisfaction with the pace and benefit of a psychoanalytic individual and group treatment over several years. A precipitant was his depressive reaction to the loss of a relationship with a woman. He described continual relationship problems, alienation from his family, and little self–definition. His religion formed a major part of the identity he possessed, but he felt that more self–development was necessary and he "didn't seem to be doing it." His love and talent resided in art, but he had committed himself to manual labor so that he could make a living wage.

Early in our sessions, he spoke of "needing a blueprint" for how to proceed with several major problems. He also brought in a recent painting. He talked about his art as a necessary channel for self-expression, more difficult for him when it was verbal and face-to-face. We talked about his beliefs and expectations relevant to various relationships. He described a bragging, somewhat manipulative interpersonal style as a means of keeping control. We talked about the meaning of control, other means of achieving it, and the need to develop the capacity to do without it some of the time.

Over a six-month period, he began liking himself more and proved able to generate some optimism. He dated, but wished for a meaningful relationship. Then an opportunity came to leave the area and join an art cooperative; he took it. He stayed for two months and then returned to Washington, resuming his labor job and psychotherapy.

Over the next six months, he continued to paint and work and date. He began to achieve his first real separation from home. A career as an artist seemed like a real possibility. Therapy again stopped, and I heard little from him for 18 months.

He returned with real concern about the absence of a committed relationship in his life. He noted how most of his peers (at 26) were married or living with someone. He put his art work on a back burner and took a job working for a relative. Psychotherapy was focused now on meanings relevant to relationship. His anger and his difficulty with trust came to the fore. After three more months of therapy, he decided to terminate.

Eighteen months later, he called to tell me about some major life changes. We scheduled a follow-up session. He had met, developed a relationship with, and would soon be engaged to marry a woman with whom he could talk. They were "a lot like each other." He had a number of career possibilities but had not yet made a commitment.

Six months later, he brought his fiancée with him for a "premarital interview." Eighteen months later, he wrote to say that marriage was going well and that they were in the midst of discussing a move out of the area. Two years later, I received a card announcing the birth of their first child. Although some (mostly career) identity questions remained, this was now a man who knew himself better, liked himself, and had taken a number of positive steps forward into life.

THE COGNITIVE WORK

In each of these cases, the relationship between therapist and patient seemed crucial. An attitude of warmth and caring, combined with a noncritical acceptance of "where the adolescent was at," permitted the therapist to be accepted as a friend. One critical difference between the parent and the therapist seemed to be the lack of real life consequence to the therapist of the patient's successes or failures. It was evident to the patients that I hoped for their success and that I tried to be comforting and encouraging when there were setbacks. However, I would not be measured in terms of their outcome.

I found that, through analogy, I talked with these patients a great deal about my own children. I felt that, if they had ever met, the appropriate greeting might be: "It's good to meet you. I have heard so much about you!" I could role model, in this way, a kind of acceptance of disappointment, a "rolling with the punches of life," as well as a pride in achievement.

By continually approaching their situations in terms of thinking (as opposed to behavior), we kept the emphasis on what they could do to affect their environment. This was meant to counter the orientation to blaming external events and listening to influential others instead of taking responsibility for themselves.

By identifying cognitive errors and thinking up alternatives, we focused on choices as opposed to "right and wrong." Over time, I believe that this helped the adolescent build a repertoire that would become him or her "self." Dwelling on displeasing outcomes was discouraged; instead, we would return to goals ("What did you want to accomplish?") and means ("How can you get there?").

Each psychotherapy had a prominent section on risk assessment, as the adolescents were encouraged to take prudent risks. This encouragement was aimed at countering the restrictions built upon the foundation of multiple avoidances over time. I would often refer to risks my children had taken in areas relevant to the issue of the moment in therapy.

At times, "talking it out with your parents" was promoted. At other times, support for the patient's growing autonomy took the path of suggesting that they keep their own counsel. I usually made it clear that I was available to them to chat "at any time." Limits were set so that weekend telephone "chats" at home were not opportunities for hour-long sessions.

The bulwark of the therapy focused on the use of the triple column. Homework was more uniform with this group than with my patients in general. It seemed to provide the additional structure that this group required. Frequently, that homework entailed the keeping of a log that formed the basis for therapeutic work in the office. That log usually catalogued situations, feelings, and automatic thoughts. This work progressed to the identification of schemas and then to the design of experiments to test the usefulness of basic rules.

I was flexible in terms of scheduling appointments with parent or parents, boy or girlfriends — fact, any significant other who the collaborating pair felt would help illuminate an issue or problem. Often, my patient and I would spend a session preparing for a future collateral visit.

Now, let me discuss one attempt at reparenting in detail to illustrate the principles. When I met Sarah she was 21 years old, living at home and being treated for depression with antidepressant medication. She was working in a bookstore, after "barely graduating" from high school. She had tried a community college but left, feeling scared and overwhelmed. She had not had a date in two years. She described her orientation to life as: "I sit around waiting for things to happen." She had experienced severe social anxiety in a variety of situations. She had had three years of psychotherapy, with little change.

Initially, we discussed common everyday problems and possible alternative approaches to them. She learned the cognitive terminology quickly and was working in the format of the triple column. Atypically, the interaction between us became an early focus for therapy because of several missed appointments, followed by a "you're mad at me" letter. When the relationship is explored in cognitive therapy, it is not understood in terms of transference. Rather, it is treated as any other situation or relationship would be. What are your feelings? And what are the associated thoughts? This approach quickly and concretely distinguished our contact and task from those between Sarah and other "adults."

When she began a dating relationship with a negative and manipulative young man, this became the third agenda item for therapy. Shortly thereafter, she took the first trip alone that she had taken in several years, and it went well. Earlier, she had avoided travel because of vague apprehensions about being alone. This represented a growth step, therefore, and we studied it in detail to identify both her thinking and her successful actions.

Her fear of vomiting and then of a dental procedure occupied us next. In each case, she emphasized the need to maintain conscious control or else feel the fear associated with losing control.

She moved out of her parents' home and got an apartment with a friend. She began to consider leaving the bookstore for a "better job." She thought about how she might gradually return to college. After six months of therapy, she was less depressed, most of the time. There was, however, little sense of who she was and little effective separation from family, with continued unsatisfactory relationship experiences with men.

Sarah registered for two courses and got a job in a clinical setting working with the elderly. Often, she refused to acknowledge her gains, fearing they would, somehow, be taken away. Her progress was "saw-toothed," with real jumps forward balanced by frequent falls backward. At several points that required a decision, suicidal ideas emerged. She understood this to mean an incapacity to cope with the consequences of choice by avoiding the decision entirely.

By the one–year anniversary of weekly psychotherapy, we began decreasing her antidepressant drug, upon which she had become psychologically dependent. In her thinking, a common cognitive error was overgeneralization. I tried to point it out whenever it came up. For example, at times she would focus on aspects of her appearance (she was extremely attractive) and find specific fault, generalizing to the belief that she was ugly.

Sarah dropped one of her two classes because it involved others scrutinizing her work and she was unwilling to permit that. In another class, she was maintaining a B average when she missed several classes and suddenly dropped out. Predictably, she generalized and lost the confidence for a time that she could do college–level work. Over a period of several weeks, she thought through the school experience and reached some more specific conclusions about the outcome of her "trial of school." She wanted to return to school, but was unclear as to the best strategy for doing it. Meanwhile, she began a rocky relationship with a man, adopting the posture of trying to please him and finding it difficult to express to him how she felt.

We scheduled a meeting for her parents, Sarah, and me. I told them about her gains in therapy in terms of identity, work, and to some extent, self-worth. They were proud of her but somewhat taken aback when I suggested that she was ready to try full-time schoolwork. They agreed to support her if she was motivated to follow this course. She was, and their support was an important boost for Sarah. By now, she no longer took any medication.

She registered for a full schedule of classes. She handled the interview and made the adaptation to college classes surprisingly easily. She was astonished that she could now express herself in a classroom setting. She moved back home to save some money.

A long-term relationship ended. Her school term also ended, with a B average. She registered for another full term. Sarah liked her clinic job, but was envious of others with credentials to work with the older residents and oriented her thinking toward a mental health job. She was now comfortable in many social settings, permitting her to identify some specific phobias, for example, one of air travel. We worked on this by identifying and testing her automatic thoughts, then considering alternatives.

When she became ill with a respiratory problem, a lengthy hospitalization raised anew some issues (dependency, separation, fear of losing her gains) which seemingly had been put behind her. There were several telephone sessions during her hospital stay, aimed at reestablishing perspective.

At the same time, she had met and begun to date a young man quite dissimilar from previous choices. It was pointed out that she, too, was hardly the same as she was five years earlier, when psychotherapy had begun. Visits were now more sporadic, usually monthly. Over time, she and her boyfriend overcame some obstacles to their relationship and deepened their commitment. She worried that "something would happen" to affect this area of happiness she had found. We traced this belief to a schema in which she told herself that she was unworthy of success in any life area. Considering this, it made little sense to her in light of the changes she had been able to make over recent years. We discussed self-confidence, and what might form a rational basis for possessing it.

She talked about school and her concern with the outcome of a particular class. Meanwhile, she acknowledged doing well in all her other classes. This particular subject required intensive work and she wondered aloud whether she was motivated to do it. We reviewed her goals in school and what she expected to gain from her degree. I asked her if in fact she felt that she was *incapable* of doing the work required or whether the issue was truly whether she *wanted* to do it. I stressed the limited time she would have to work hard to master this subject and how important it was for her that she knew she *could* achieve in this class if she chose to.

She saw a future issue in the need to learn to accept those aspects of the style of her boyfriend that were different from hers. She talked of career issues involved in finding a first "definitive" job. Another area that required continued work was her tendency to make arbitrary inferences about low probability events, and then to take them personally.

In the months that followed, appointments were less frequent. The young couple planned their wedding, and Sarah started her last school term. There were multiple occasions upon which she "spoke her mind," previously a difficult challenge for her. She overreacted to a class exercise by personalizing it, and then loosened its grip on her by discussing it with a variety of people. Now that she was truly "somebody," it was okay to share even the rough edges of herself with significant others. We worked to differentiate what belonged to the "old Sarah" and might occasionally recur from those areas that would require continued vigilance and work for her to feel good. I remarked, on many occasions, how rewarding it was for me to see the person she had "become." She felt not quite like a daughter, not quite like an adult peer. I always looked forward to our now infrequent sessions.

Five years had passed and Sarah had achieved some self-definition. She had completed her schooling and had begun to actively look for a job. She had met and married a man who fit her concept of a "mate for life." She was a functioning member of a loving family, but was busy now establishing a family of her own. She had a real feeling of having successfully negotiated a difficult life passage. She seemed ready to confront the challenges and uncertainties of life that lay ahead. Those adaptive qualities of sensitivity, hard work, and loyalty that she had been taught by her family early in life were now evident, unobstructed by the obstacles of depression and anxiety.

11
Couples Therapy

I don't deliberately treat couples very often. Sometimes, though, I commit myself to a person who has clear communication problems with a spouse. The "couples therapy," therefore, evolves as a second stage of an individual treatment. I also see significant others as part of an evaluation often enough so that I have gotten to know (at least a little bit) some husbands and wives of my patients.

More is involved when a second party is introduced into the therapy than merely providing another chair in the room. When the initial treatment was individual, the entering spouse may logically consider the therapy pair as "bonded" in some way. At the least, the therapist has had contact with and learned about one person in detail. He or she has formed an impression of that person and likely identified some admirable qualities. They may have achieved some success together, paving the way for an attempt to work with the marital pair.

The spouse may believe that he or she has already been represented in the therapy, perhaps unfairly. The view of the spouse has been presented (distorted?) within the context of another's needs, beliefs, and meanings. How can the therapist now be unbiased and helpful to the couple? Won't he or she support the views of his patient against those of the spouse? These considerations make the success of a venture proceeding from individual to couples therapy less likely. And, to be fair, at times this procedure does not work well. A new therapist, meeting the couple afresh, may have real advantages.

However, at times the good relationship with the initial patient is not seen as an obstacle, but rather as a benefit. The patient may have shared with the spouse much of the content of the therapy sessions. The therapist may have been presented to the spouse as a source of support, rather than as an adversary. He or she may be seen as a "family friend." Several patients have told me that their spouses were not motivated to "start with someone new," but that they were willing to see me because they believed that they would he comfortable and "familiar with how I operate."

Aside from considering the meanings to each person of events in the therapy, applying the cognitive model to work with couples appears to offer few additional problems. Once again, the model provides a language within which to understand the interpersonal difficulties of two people. Often, I have found, the hard work of one member seems to spur the other to work hard as well.

One couple I encountered years ago is particularly memorable. Rather than meeting and treating one first, with the couples therapy following, I shifted back and forth between individual and couples work. In prospect this would seem to offer maximal opportunity for disruption and discontinuity, with little chance for success. In practice, I believe it worked optimally for each partner, as well as for the partnership.

Rebecca came with her husband for an initial evaluation. She told me that she and Robert had problems talking about things, but more urgently, that she had "stopped functioning" in her usual manner. Robert was an attorney in the small town in which they lived. For many years, Rebecca had organized and managed his office. They had raised three "smart, good children."

Twelve years earlier, he had changed the focus of his practice and she did what today would be called paralegal work. Eight years ago, they consulted their family doctor because of their communication problem and had 10 joint sessions with him over a three-month period. Three years ago, Robert's practice decreased in volume, Rebecca got a job as a secretary to someone else, and he felt abandoned. She felt pretty good. Only later did her depression manifest. For the past six months, they had tried to deal with the consequences of her leaving the practice, with little success.

She described herself as a 50-year-old woman who seeks approval, avoids anger, needs autonomy, is generally passive, and makes considerable demands on herself. She felt that she had not accomplished much in life thus far and often seemed to have little time for herself.

Over the past six months, she had experienced disrupted sleep, awakening in the middle of the night, and again earlier than necessary in the morning. She felt a tightness in her throat, a loss of appetite, a decrease in energy, constant fatigue, and poor concentration. She had sustained a 20–pound weight loss. In sum, she described a chronic depression, with acute symptoms becoming prominent over the past six months.

She had not led a sheltered life. Born in Maine, she left home to attend nursing school in Texas. She became a nurse in a small town, then joined the Navy and was abroad for five years. She met her husband abroad, married and moved to a small town in Virginia. They had three children and, as they all grew older, she worked in her husband's practice.

Robert was 49 years old. His father, too, had been an attorney. Born in a small town in Ohio, he attended college in the midwest and law school in Boston. He met his wife while in the Army in Germany. He was attracted to her physically, and stressed that he liked her independence.

He saw the marriage as bringing each of them some fun and the chance to travel together, as well as three fine children and untold hours spent together. They had worked in the same space for years and now he knew that she needed more distance. The marriage, despite its many positive aspects, had provided little feedback for him, little real "contact." He knew she didn't easily tell him how she felt and that often she felt "inferior."

Robert was action-oriented and extroverted. His relationship with Rebecca was very important to him and he found that he missed terribly her physical presence at work. At the initial evaluation, his major problem seemed to be an interpersonal (relationship) one, while Rebecca had a depression that required immediate attention. I decided to treat her individually first.

She began the initial session by describing her identity as "totally wrapped up in Robert and the practice." She desperately wanted to be herself, "whatever that was." She wanted to do something "all her own." In subsequent meetings, she described a life filled with "shoulds." We discussed rational parameters for her self-worth, how she assessed risk before acting, what were her choices, and whether there was any benefit in her expressing "minority opinions."

She became aware, over time, of some anger at Robert. I took this as a cue to invite her husband "into the therapy" and began to identify with them an agenda for the couple. In the first joint session, they demonstrated to each other how each of their concepts of "spouse" was seriously flawed. Also, their temperaments and styles were substantially different. She was, by now (two months into therapy) becoming less depressed. I assured Robert that she could tolerate his anger and disappointment with her and encouraged him to express it. Likewise, she permitted herself to get angry with him.

He found it difficult to "take risks" with her, hard to allow himself to become vulnerable. His overriding expressed concern was a fear of hurting her with his words. As she became more open, he was able to take more risks. By the fourth joint meeting, they reported less tension at home and more "cross-talk." Now, a dominant issue was determining what Rebecca wanted out of life and facilitating her achievement of that goal.

Toward that end, I scheduled several individual sessions with Rebecca. She identified some negative automatic thoughts:

1. "I do it differently, and I'm wrong."
2. "When he feels sad, I feel responsible."
3. "I expect him to do as I do."

The cognitions were challenged, and I told Rebecca that she needed a better guide to understand Robert than she would find by her own example. She reported continuing recovery from depression and was now ready to decide whether she wanted to return to Robert's office or to continue at her present job. She worried about not having any autonomy if she returned, but acknowledged that she was now better able to express her wishes to Robert. She, too, missed the "special time" their work together had provided.

Six months after therapy began, she decided to rejoin the law practice. They brought me a gift, a blackboard, which I have since used on a daily basis. ("Every cognitive therapist needs a blackboard," Rebecca said.) We discussed two levels of communicating: a focus on content and a focus on process. At any point, either

Rebecca or Robert could make a comment to the other on either level.

They worked hard, separately and together, between sessions. Rebecca described a trap that she set for herself. "If I do what I want to do," she said, "I may get what I want, risk provoking Robert's anger and then feel guilty. If I don't do what I want, I won't get what I want and then will put myself down for it. The way I see it, I lose either way," she said.

"I, too, have a trap," Robert said. "I avoid telling her what I think because she may do what I want in order to get my approval. Or, she won't do what I want in order to assert her independence. I lose either way," he said.

Each could see in listening to the other how one's cognitive set paved the way to the trap. The solution involved first challenging the expectation and then faithfully representing to each other their real needs. Once again, Rebecca was confronting her sense of responsibility for her husband's happiness. And Robert needed to learn to accept his wife as a person in her own right. By the next joint session, they each expressed an awareness of movement. He began to think of her statements as "trial balloons." She saw her main issue as choosing between freedom and responsibility.

With Rebecca scheduled for minor surgery, I planned my first individual session with Robert. He reported feeling "more understood" by her. He felt she was "gaining inner strength." As a group of three, there was a growing friendship among Robert, Rebecca, and me.

A decidedly more optimistic Rebecca turned up for the next few individual sessions, but now she thought that Robert was becoming depressed. She attributed his mood change to his "seeing her slipping away" and fearing that she would leave him. He had expressed to her a need for a few "private lessons with me."

I scheduled a few individual sessions with Robert. He described the phenomenon as "twinning," his expectation that Rebecca would be like him. I compared their style difference (each effective, parallel roads to Rome) to the differing color of their eyes. We discussed in detail the consequences of accepting one's spouse despite (or because of) the differences.

Rebecca and I then met individually. She discussed two important issues that she felt she was dealing with effectively: conveying her sexual needs to Robert and dealing with a daughter's college choice. When next the spouses came together, they jointly lamented how they seemed to be moving in opposite directions. He was looking to leave the practice of law to move on to something else. She was looking to find a career to form part of a new identity. Over a short time, she came to the conclusion that work wasn't *necessary* for her to have an identity, and wouldn't suffice for one, either.

They spent a fun vacation together, the first in many years. She reported "liking him again" and no longer fearing that she would imminently become depressed. Robert, who enjoyed sailing as a hobby, quoted Seneca: "For the man who has no harbor, no wind is a good wind." He was focusing now on a career change that threatened his self-worth equation. Rebecca noted how multiple options presented themselves to her in most situations now, where there used to be only "shoulds."

Now, one year after therapy began, the couple came in and each told of a return of depressive feelings. "I am nothing, feel phony, empty and weak," she said. She had found an old diary and relived her past negative thinking. She had been "fooling" me and her husband into believing things were now different. Nothing had really changed. Robert told of having few friends. His self-confidence was diminished because his "children were leaving, his wife no longer needed him, his practice was disappearing, and he was faced with the loss of Rebecca as a partner."

I talked with them about being "stuck in the same old x–y axis." It was time to shift their focus to the rules (the process) rather than battling with the content. In response, they each re–framed their dominant view as a "crisis of confidence," as opposed to "their plight." Each acknowledged that they had distorted their appraisal of the gains achieved in the past year to fit a reaction of the moment. Robert emphasized his need to look inside himself for guidance to life's next stage. Rebecca pointed to how important it was for her that she and her husband have a "common identity" in addition to her own. One unexpected consequence of Rebecca's return to the practice for both of them was an insight into how working together now was not the same as it was before. Neither found it as satisfying as was anticipated.

Eighteen months after therapy began, Rebecca no longer had signs of depression. She had quit her job and "returned home" to an uncertain future in the practice. She felt it was the right thing to do for herself. Robert had learned to "have input" without exercising total control, He told of "getting a glimpse 25 years later of 'the girl' I married."

In the last session, we reviewed formally what each of us saw as having transpired in therapy. They stressed the "unique relationship" we three had shared. She saw major changes in herself, having been put in touch with her resources. Robert described a loosening and relaxation of an essentially obsessive-compulsive style. He could more easily relinquish control and relax now, in a new way. He remained unclear about his career direction, but felt confident he would find a "rewarding port in which to drop anchor."

I am not suggesting that, for any individual psychotherapy, the patient's spouse can easily be shuttled into and out of the treatment room. Most clinical cautions have some sound reasoning as their basis. I have found, however, that there are potential advantages as well as potential disadvantages to this clinical "sequencing." While issues of maintaining confidentiality and siding with one of a pair may defeat this arrangement, the good will generated with one family member may present dividends in the engagement of another. With gains for each of two individuals added to the growth of the couple, the outcome validated an attempt at therapeutic flexibility.

For those clinicians with a special interest in marital therapy, a new book by Beck, *Love is Never Enough*[9] presents cognitive strategies and interventions that may augment your clinical repertoire.

12
Follow–up

The mission of the University of Pennsylvania's psychiatry program was to train academicians. Their graduates would teach and do research, treating enough patients to maintain living contact with their subject of inquiry. We were taught that every patient was an "n of one" research study, worthy of considerable thought and likely to contribute ideas to the treatment of subsequent patients.

This approach led naturally to keeping detailed records, to noting hypotheses whether or not they proved to be correct, and to using rating scales for more quantitative measurement of significant variables. While a resident in training, I was encouraged to terminate a psychotherapy treatment properly by considering what had happened in the therapy, why change had occurred when it did, and what the nuances were of ending the relationship between therapist and patient.

It was evident to me that most therapists never again see their patients after psychotherapy is over, unless there is a call for more treatment and the patient chooses to resume with the same therapist. However, I had been taught that this leads to a lack of understanding by the therapist of where the treatment fit in the context of the patient's life. Surely, a patient who subsequently found another therapist, may have received medication, may have required inpatient treatment, or may have found success in another modality of therapy had reached a different outcome from one who applied what he had learned over a period of months or years, with success and without further consultation. Similarly, someone who had a few booster sessions ("reminders") of the therapy approach at key times in the future was in a different outcome category from one who had several lengthy periods of therapeutic contact. It seems obvious that there is no way to know this at the time therapy ends.

In this framework, my commitment to follow–up was nurtured. I would suggest to my patient, after all but the briefest of contacts, that we meet again one month after termination. In a flexible program, a subsequent meeting would usually be set for three months later and then for three or six months after that. I was told many times that a follow-up program facilitated the patient's initiative in calling me at a time of future need. It implied continuing interest. In addition, for most people having problems subsequent to a period of psychotherapy, a short course recalling the cognitive approach, one session in the office or one chat on the telephone, led to successful problem–solving.

Early in my psychotherapy experience, a depressed man successfully completed about 20 sessions and resolved his mid-life problem. For follow-up, I saw him three times over the following year, in what would become my standard paradigm. Toward the end of our "final, final session," he asked why we needed to stop. He had found these periodic "life and coping" reviews to be useful. He made the analogy to car care, "If I am willing to bring my automobile to the dealer every 10,000 miles for routine maintenance," he said, "why shouldn't I take similar care of myself?" In this way, the concept of follow-up as an "oil and lube" for the cognitive apparatus was born. We made a contract to meet every six months, until he decided that it served no further useful purpose. We met six times over a three–year period.

A significant number of people I have treated return, at some point, for more therapeutic work. Several have recalled to me my standard departing statement: "Remember, if you run into an obstacle you cannot deal with alone, you now have an account at Chase Manhattan. Call me, and we will determine together what will meet your needs."

Colleagues have told me that few clients or patients would be willing to pay for therapy when they are functioning well. I have found just the opposite to be true. The follow-up program is often seen as an insurance policy against the possibility of future incapacitating problems,

For the therapist, the gains in follow–up are potentially enormous. I have been able to differentiate those who have learned and applied the cognitive model successfully from those who feel better at the end of therapy but have *learned* little of lasting value. I have identified a group of relapsing depressives (for example) whose problem seems to be biologically based and whose course seems impervious to psychological learning. Especially in these patients, and in some less seriously ill as well, there are characteristics inherent in learning that occur in one state (for example, "well") that do not transfer to another state (for example, "ill"). This state–dependent learning can defeat the patient's attempt to apply gains in psychotherapy to abort subsequent depressive reactions. A final benefit for the therapist comes from intermixing a few follow-up sessions with relatively well individuals with those draining hours spent with the acutely ill.

The structure for these follow-up hours is fairly well established in my practice. Following the initial greeting, "It's good to see you again" (and if it isn't good to be together again, the patient usually won't come!), we review events and circumstances over the elapsed period. We note emotional symptoms and recurrent problems. The format most commonly employed utilizes a triple column structure. I remind the patient of the cognitive therapy approach and together we apply it to situations and reactions. Even if there have been several emergent problems, a detailed application in therapy to one of them often permits the patient to take on additional issues by him or herself. The session ends with a plan for further contact at my initiative at a specified time, or at the patient's calling as needed.

A REVIEW OF FINDINGS AT
FOLLOW-UP

Joan, a 25–year–old, unmarried woman, consulted me after becoming depressed while on a vacation trip. Her first episode of depression had occurred five years earlier, accompanied by a serious suicide attempt. She was not now suicidal, but did score 18 (of a maximum 39) on a short form of the Beck Depression Inventory,[25] a score consistent with severe depression. I treated her with an antidepressant drug (Desipramine, 150 mgms. per day) and cognitive therapy.

Psychotherapy consisted of 10 sessions over a 10–week period.

The focus was on a recent relationship that had gone awry. We considered her need to grieve the loss, her continuing need for his approval, her anger at how he treated her, and her negative self-view. As her depression cleared, she was able to learn to be more assertive with her wants and expressive of her feelings. She gradually reoriented her self-view, detaching it from the input of her recent boyfriend.

When I saw her two weeks after the course of therapy was complete, she talked about pressure from her old boyfriend to resume their relationship. She told him that she "still cared for him" but was not interested in a reconciliation. She was dieting and had managed to lose seven pounds over a three-week period.

When I saw her one month later, she felt "good to be alive" and remarked that she was now "letting people know how she felt on a regular basis." Three months later, she had sustained her gains and her BDI score was zero. A new relationship had begun and "blossomed." She was sleeping well and was energetic, taking now a maintenance dose of Desipramine.

Three months still later, her relationship, job, and self-esteem were all doing well. We discontinued the medication. A telephone call one year later revealed no recurrence of depression. The follow-up program permitted some conclusions to be stated with confidence. I believe that her depression responded to a course of antidepressant medication and that she had made good use of a short-term cognitive therapy to make some adjustments in her thinking about relationships.

Dave, a 35-year-old man, married with two small children, presented with complaints about the rigidity of his obsessive-compulsive style. He had a history of alcoholism, and he and his wife had once had couples therapy after he had disclosed an extramarital affair. Their therapist suggested that he find some individual treatment to complement the couples work.

We discussed the disparity between his expectations for himself and his achievements, his difficulty with openness and intimacy, and his problems acknowledging dependency and feelings. This was accomplished within the context of a cognitive approach based upon the triple column technique.

He became better able to enjoy a social occasion without alcohol. He found it easier to talk in therapy about what angered him. During one part of the almost nine–month course of treatment, he noted real difficulty in handling feelings of which, in the past, he had been unaware. He began to cultivate interests outside of work. At another point, he emphasized that he found the "repetitiveness" of therapy hard to tolerate.

Late in our time together, his son expressed anger at "not seeing enough of daddy." Dave supported the observation and made significant schedule changes in response to it. He saw himself as "much more flexible" and "much less uptight." He saw workaholism as a danger to avoid.

Two weeks after our "last" session, he noted that, for the first time in memory, he was pleased with himself. He reviewed how he was dealing with the major areas of his life.

One month later, he described a "new willingness to share himself with others." He was now able to "have some fun." He told me how difficult it had been for him to accept the suggestion of individual psychotherapy and how glad be was that he had come. He would miss the "social aspect" of our work together.

Dave called 18 months later to set up an appointment. The stimulus of a job offer had led to a return of "old thinking." On a blackboard, we outlined in detail his thinking concerning the meanings inherent in his accepting a new position. One session proved sufficient for him to reestablish perspective.

Three years later, he called during a period of self-appraisal, triggered by some new work opportunities. He was so attuned to the needs of those around him that, he felt, his own needs were getting lost. He was considering marital separation. We agreed to a brief course of cognitive therapy focusing on his marital decision. Over a six–week period, Dave successfully resolved his doubts and recommitted himself to the relationship with his wife. I believe that our relationship, nurtured through follow–up, facilitated a successful brief therapy years later for a man otherwise unlikely to have sought consultation.

Phil, a man in his mid–thirties, consulted me 10 weeks after his wife had left him. He blamed himself for her departure and stated, "Right now, I don't like myself very much." He had many obsessive traits and found it hard to express anger.

By our second session, his wife had decided that he should have custody of their daughter Annie, age 4. He talked about how angry he was at his wife and how anxious he was about assuming the burdens of single parenthood.

By the seventh session, he felt confused by his wife's behavior and by her decisions. Soon he was made aware of her relationship with another man, and of her plan to leave the area and settle elsewhere. By session 15, he had recovered the bases for his self-worth, accepted his expanded parental role, and resumed many of his prior behaviors.

We made an appointment for one month later, after a discussion of issues relevant to termination. At that time, he had begun a new relationship and deepened his tie (and time) with his daughter. We had several follow-up sessions at monthly intervals. Relationships came and went. He was alternately irritated by and delighted with the demands and antics of his daughter. During a time when everything appeared to be changing, the follow-up sessions were a useful anchor for him.

A meeting after the passage of six months revealed an obsessive man who had weathered a challenging situation after an initial adjustment problem and was now attacking life with his previous verve. He was more aware of and expressive with his feelings, and his young daughter remained the first priority of his life. For him, follow-up provided a useful bridge to a life of difficult and novel circumstances.

Susan, a woman in her late thirties, was referred to me by an old friend and colleague when she became acutely depressed. A perfectionist by nature, she viewed most problems through a polarized (black and white) lens. She desperately sought the approval of a rejecting parent who had led a radically different life from that chosen by her daughter. She didn't know how to relax or how to spend free time.

Psychotherapy centered around the concept of choices and consequences. Cognitive errors (chiefly personalization and polarization) were consistently identified, and alternative strategies were developed for approaching situations. She recovered from the acute depression and made significant gains at work and at home over a five-month period. The follow-up sessions reemphasized the cognitive method for her.

Over a six-month period, she called twice for sessions aimed at helping her cope with brief absences of her husband related to his job. Her problems concerned feelings and beliefs of dependency and a host of "what-if's" that were generating anxiety.

One year after termination, she returned for a second course of psychotherapy, precipitated by the birth of a child and her transition from full-time work to full-time parenting. She felt "trapped" and overwhelmed. Her self-view, previously tied to work success, was taking a beating as she tried to establish herself at home. This therapy, lasting three months, facilitated a life stage transition for her.

Monthly phone calls charted a continuing good adaptation, until a proposed job transfer for her husband precipitated a third course of therapy. Three sessions were devoted to helping her establish an acceptable meaning for what had transpired. Having been born in the midwest and having moved to Washington, she would now reside in Massachusetts. In this short contact, real impediments to the couple's communication were revealed. I believe that my continuing contact with her over this two–and–one–half–year period facilitated the scheduling of several very helpful joint sessions at this time.

Susan's husband, Stephen (with whom I had had only brief telephone conversation), joined the therapy with surprising ease (see Chapter 11). He revealed that he felt he "had known me for a long time" before we finally had the opportunity to meet. There were no preliminaries, and we set right to the task of pinpointing their communication problem. Susan seemed proud of Stephen's "ease" in therapy, and pleased that the two of us could finally meet. She felt confident that, reasoning together, we would soon find a solution. Stephen knew the cognitive method from some preparatory reading he had done, as well as from conversations with his wife. She expressed her anger to him about feeling excluded from his decision–making process. He asked her how he could atone for the regrettable error he had made in not involving her from the outset in the process of relocation.

The family moved to Massachusetts and several lengthy, warm letters followed. About one year later, Susan called requesting a "telephone appointment." She was having a "crisis of confidence" and the option of starting psychotherapy with someone new was

not attractive to her. Besides, she "only needed a brushup" to regain some lost perspective.

A letter one year later described a functional family, two satisfying jobs, and two growing children. Their adaptation to New
England was proceeding "on course." The therapist in Washington
was granted "honorary family membership" and offered a place to
stay while visiting the region.

V

The Model in Practice

M────13
rs. A.

This is a time of change and uncertainty for psychotherapists in general and psychiatrists in particular. Twenty years ago, I was taught, both formally and informally, a series of rules and expectations to guide my future work. Several of the realities upon which these were based have changed. The future appears to promise still further changes. Before I describe some typical cases, let me consider some of the realities that affect the model in practice.

GENERAL CONSIDERATIONS

Cognitive therapy is accorded more of an equal status with other models in psychological training than it is in the training of a psychiatrist or a social worker. Not surprisingly, I have been told many times that, although I seem knowledgeable about drug therapy and concerned about diagnosis, I "think more like" a psychologist than a psychiatrist. In many psychiatric residency programs today, the cognitive model is presented as something that "others do" and that "you should know about," but not as something you might choose to do yourself. At Georgetown University Medical School in the early 1980s, I was asked to design and teach a course in the cognitive model for the psychiatric residents. The fundamental learning experience called "Principles of Psychotherapy" was taught by a noted psychoanalyst and considered to be the course that taught you your trade.

My confusion resulting from using a "psychologist's model" as a psychiatrist is compounded by the field's ferment in deciding who, with what background, is qualified to do what kind of work. Should psychologists admit patients to hospital? Prescribe medications? And if so, would the two disciplines then be interchangeable? Should psychiatrists be restricted to treating only the severest of the mentally ill? As I write, and the decade of the nineties begins, there are questions, but no resolution.

As if the intrafamilial squabbling among colleagues isn't disturbing enough, there is the clash with the "regulators," ostensibly representing the best interests of our patients or clients. Should an insurance company or utilization reviewer determine for me how my patient is best treated? Is a health maintenance organization (HMO) the best model to insure state–of–the–art treatment for a patient with an emotional disorder?

I am skeptical that quality care will result from the new regulation. Surely, there will be less long–term treatment and more brief therapy. This will discourage some abuse related to the inappropriate prescription of lengthy psychotherapy when brief treatment would suffice. It will also deprive some people of the long–term treatment necessary for change. Strong representation of a viewpoint promoting cost effectiveness is good. When the power to decide is vested there, however, the hired personnel must be knowledgeable, flexible, and up–to–date, so that patients will be directed toward appropriate care. From what I have seen so far, I have not been impressed that this is happening. A key variable once again is who, with what background and bias, will decide.

What has changed in the past 20 years? Training in psychotherapy often does not prepare the student to meet the demands of the real world once he or she assumes the role of clinician. Establishing a working concept for multidisciplined members of the mental health treatment team has become critical, especially as the differences appear to be blurring. Learning how to talk with "the regulators" so as not to alienate them and occasionally to teach or learn from them has become a necessary skill for today's clinician.

The current chairman of psychiatry at Georgetown, Richard Goldberg, designed a course in 1981 called "Transition to Practice." He and I co-taught it as a vehicle to prepare senior residents to confront some of the issues facing them as new psychiatrists. It was forward–looking at the time; by now it should be widely available in training programs for all clinicians.

THE NONHUMAN ENVIRONMENT

I believe strongly that the ambience of a psychiatrist's office tells the prospective patient a lot about the situation he or she is about to enter. Utilizing the cognitive model, I am not uncomfortable about conveying a bit of myself in my office. The dividend for me is a comfortable, enjoyable work environment.

It's convenient to have an office close to home. I rarely walk, but it's less than a five–minute drive, with lots of places to park. I have shared a suite with another psychiatrist and a psychologist for over 10 years. We see each other briefly and surprisingly infrequently. Whoever gets here earliest picks the waiting room radio station for the day and heats water for coffee or tea. This room is small. On top of a stack of chairs sits a little wicker basket that collects our mail.

My office room represents me in a number of revealing ways to my patients. There is a pink poster from a Jerusalem Film Festival and a Matisse poster of a young woman from a Washington National Gallery of Art exhibit. Between two small chairs and a larger chair, there is a playful Rousseau poster of monkeys and oranges in the jungle. Framed photographs of Mt. Sinai and of a Pacific Northwest Indian totem pole border one window (both mine).

A colorful three–stage painting of the opening of a flower (an original Lucille Herman) sits above my desk. On the desk, in addition to telephone and answering machine, there's an open "Far Side" calendar, my Red Sea rock, a white fossil, and a jar of beach sand and shells (this vessel used to contain M & M's; however, since breaking my bag–a–day after lunch habit, I use it to maintain my covenant with the beach). A paperweight is a kindergarten gift from my younger daughter. Near one (of two) filing cabinets is a small Charles Bragg rendering of a seedy psychiatrist, complete with rabbit's foot, lucky horseshoe, and sand timer. There is a digital clock and a box of tissues, but there is no couch.

The bookcase features works of both professional and personal interest, hardback and paperback editions. There are numerous collected doodads and several greeting cards (one from my mother received on the opening of the office). There is a prominent collection of hockey pucks, one from each of 16 cities in which I have seen the NHL Washington Capitals play.

CASE EXAMPLE

Throughout the book, I have included case material and anecdotes to illustrate the cognitive model and the system of cognitive therapy. In this final section, I will describe three cases, the first of longer duration and the last two relatively brief. If doubt persists about how the model is used in practice, I hope that these chapters will answer your questions. I do not maintain that any of these three people could not have been treated utilizing a different approach; each, however, has benefited from cognitive therapy.

Mrs. A. is a 35-year-old woman, now separated from her husband of 18 years for about one year. She has two children: a son, 15 and a daughter, 17. She works for a large corporation as a secretary.

Her presenting complaint was that there was "no direction to her life." Her husband was the focal point of her concern. He was addicted to drugs and alcohol. They had been separated twice before, only to reconcile each time. Together, they no longer had a love relationship or a social life as a couple. Apart, she felt insecure, dependent, depressed, and adrift. Earlier, she lived a life that was quite isolated in a rural area, unable to drive a car, with few friends and two children to care for. He worked, traveled, and had a social group that he kept for himself.

Six years ago she got a driver's license, was hired as a secretary, and had an "office affair." Two years ago, she insisted that her husband seek treatment. One year ago, she asked him to leave. Over the past year, however, she has continued to "date" him several times a week. She claimed that when her husband was at his worst, she was most attracted to him.

She blamed herself for the "failed marriage," was ridden with guilt about his continuing addiction, had experienced sudden crying spells, been withdrawn, had suicidal ideas, and felt helpless over the six months prior to coming to my office. She had no physical symptoms of depression.

Her father was alcoholic and had taken several overdoses of drugs. Her mother divorced her father when my patient was an infant and later married a "severe and distant man." She was the third of four children.

She described herself as "nice, cares about people, successful at work." She identified as central to her self-worth, "what I could do to help my husband." Her goals for the psychotherapy were:

1. To understand why she stayed with her husband.
2. To be able to fully separate from him.
3. To change a low self-image.

My initial diagnostic impression was dysthymic disorder (chronic depression). During the initial sessions, she talked mostly about her husband and her guilt at "not being able to do enough for him." An early homework assignment was to keep a record of the things she had done for herself during the week.

While her list did have several entries, she acknowledged that "all stopped after he had called her, and her attention thereafter was riveted on him." I suggested that she look at her husband's behavior with regard to how it reflected *his* needs. She responded, "He wants to be taken care of, and I need to be nurturing."

For several sessions we focused on her part in maintaining the marital relationship. Some of the beliefs identified were:

1. She saw herself as inadequate.
2. She felt worth "so much less" than her husband.
3. She was angry with him.
4. She stayed connected to him "for security."
5. She "owed him" support and continued help.

We worked to identify cognitive errors and then to generate alternative views of their relationship and how it was maintained. As she developed a more realistic appraisal of her marriage, new beliefs emerged:

1. She feared being alone.
2. She feared the loss of the protection he gave her.
3. She believed she would never find someone else.

These cognitions were examined critically.

I suggested that she purchase and read the book *Feeling Good*.[29] She began to redefine the degree of rational responsibility she had for the conduct of her husband's life. We discussed what she could do for herself, and she decided to take up a new form of exercise. She took social initiative with a female friend at work.

After two months of therapy, she considered the possibility of a relationship with another man. Her basic belief was, "I am uninteresting and won't be attractive to anyone." We discussed the validity of her view. Where there were deficits, we each suggested potential remedies. She feared taking the risk of meeting a man. "It will be the wrong type of relationship," she said. We formed a balance sheet on the issue of an active versus a passive approach to social life.

I told her the story of "the little blond boy" (which is an adaptation of "the little blonde girl theory"). The origin of the theory traces to my third year in medical school. Asleep in the middle of a cold winter night, I heard a knock on my dorm room door. The door then opened, and in walked the loveliest looking blonde girl I had ever seen. She lingered briefly, then turned and left. I awoke the next morning, unsure about whether my recollection was of reality or a dream.

When I tell this story, the punch line is aimed at illustrating the probability of acquiring a lasting relationship in this passive fashion. I sometimes summarize all the reasons that make this desired outcome an unlikely one. The polar opposite alternative requires a good deal of ingenuity and assertiveness. In the middle ground, the person desiring to meet a significant other puts him or herself in places that increase the probability of the desired outcome. Preferably, these are places that reflect an interest or a pleasure of the patient, making it likely that someone met there might share this in common. And, if no one turns up, the experience can be pleasurable nevertheless.

After three months of therapy, she noted feeling more energy and less depression and being less preoccupied with thoughts of her husband. She summarized neatly the basic orientation of our approach: "The whole process is in reorienting your thinking," she said."You put yourself in others' shoes sometimes, instead of always focusing on yourself."

Christmas was approaching, and she noticed a lowering of mood in anticipation of the holiday. She identified the relevant belief: "The vacation is a test of how I do, with my kids and without my husband. I will have failed if the kids don't have a great time." We discussed the concept of distinguishing the controllable from the uncontrollable.

When she met an old boyfriend and found him unsuitable, she thought, "I can't have a relationship with any man." This was labeled an overgeneralization, and the reasons *she* didn't want a relationship with *him* were identified and seemed quite realistic. Another belief, "I don't know how to be a single person," led to a discussion of risk-taking. The identification of a system that wildly overestimated degree of risk was linked to an unreasonable set of self-standards. The error of catastrophizing was frequent in this context.

Five months into therapy, she heard about a new female friend of her husband, and thought, "I am alone, rejected and inadequate." Further, she believed, "I had hoped that someday we'd be together again." We discussed her marital relationship as it might look to her ten years from now.

After six months, she began regularly taking social initiative with both women and men. She noted how much better she felt now than she did when we started. She identified the schema of her need for approval from others. At this point, her husband made an unannounced visit to her house while she had a male visitor. She felt embarrassed and vulnerable. We worked for two sessions on her thinking, the errors, and alternatives. She later referred to this work as the "turning point in achieving some control over my life."

She took a long-postponed vacation to the beach, and brought the photos in for me to see. She helped a fellow employee with an alcohol problem, reminding herself of the stresses associated with living with her husband.

Mrs. A. decided to move, bought a house and sold her own. She assertively told a prospective employer during a job interview that his unreasonably high expectations for employees might account for the high rate of turnover he had experienced with his workers. She got the job. She discussed issues related to "letting go" of her now 18–year–old daughter.

After eight months of therapy, we began to discuss termination. "I have gotten the tools I needed," she said. "I can initiate things and am less fearful of taking risks. By sharing with me things you've done [self-disclosure], it made you more human, and I felt that we were at the same level. I know better now who I am and what resources I have." She and her husband signed a separation agreement.

She greeted me one week later with the words: "We can stop now." She felt that she had handled an intermittent problem effectively. She knew that there would be more problems as life went on, but she felt capable of representing herself well. We agreed to meet for two follow-up sessions, after one month intervals. She sent me a letter several months following her last session. She felt that she had achieved a great deal. Her divorce was now final. She enjoyed her new, challenging job and her new home. She had an active social life and felt that she had "changed some of the basis for her self-worth." She saw herself as more independent, assertive, and able to take reasonable risks. She was no longer depressed.

$M_{r. B.}$ $\overline{}^{14}$

Those who treat the severely impaired sometimes deride their colleagues for concentrating on clients or patients with "problems in living." It makes sense to me, using a psychoeducational model of therapy, that some healthy individuals may be confronted with a problem they cannot solve and will profit from brief therapy. This therapy often helps them resolve the immediate problem and, equally important, teaches an approach that may be useful in facing subsequent situations. Such was the case with Mr. B.

Mr. B. was a 30–year–old engineer, married for about 10 years, who had been employed by the same firm for almost five years. He returned from a vacation noticing that he was unusually nervous upon awakening in the morning, had little appetite, and had pain in his abdomen. He consulted his family physician who discovered that he had hypertension and prescribed appropriate medication, dietary regulation, and an exercise regimen. Having taken the time to discuss in detail with him his work dissatisfaction she noted multiple work stressors and additional physical symptoms of stress. She suggested that he consult a psychiatrist, but not for traditional "treatment"; rather, she advised, he needed to learn to better identify and cope with stress. Failure to change might result in additional and disabling medical problems.

Mr. B.'s father was a college professor who had earlier suffered a heart attack. His mother was a homemaker whom he described as a "worrier." When he came to see me, Mr. B. described a distant but not distressing relationship with his parents and a wonderful rapport with his wife. His painting and sculpting hobbies brought him real satisfaction, although they were one arena in which his perfectionism was evident. There seemed to be little to work on until he described his job.

Five years ago, he had joined a small engineering firm where his contributions were highly respected. He was given little direction or structure. He felt the firm often squandered money and worked inefficiently. He believed that they held their employees to a fairly low standard of output, well below his own. He wanted to look elsewhere for a job. The "situation," however (location, benefits, relatively nondemanding environment), was hard to relinquish. Management certainly wanted him to stay. Often, however, he was asked to turn in work he believed was still far from completion in order to meet an arbitrary deadline. "They" were most satisfied with his work, but he was not and he would argue for an extension of time. It usually was refused.

My impression, after the evaluation, was of a man with an obsessive-compulsive style who was having psychosomatic symptoms of stress. I believed that teaching him the cognitive method might provide him with an additional tool for stress reduction.

I suggested that he read *Feeling Good*[29] for a quick exposure to the cognitive method. In our second session, he told me that it did not seem useful because "he was not depressed." I realized then that my approach had to be more concrete and directly relevant to his complaint. I outlined the principles of the model for him, using his work issues to generate the content. We worked on understanding the meanings to him of uncertainty and lack of control in work situations. He defined for me his minimally acceptable self-standards.

One week later, we focused on his expectations and those of others for him in the work setting. We discussed the concept of "taking responsibility for outcomes" as opposed to "doing his best." In the following session, he noted that he was catching and challenging successfully some perfectionistic notions. He contrasted his capacity to control his hobby-work ("If I'm doing a painting for someone else and it's not done to my satisfaction," he said, "I just call them up and tell them that it will be delayed.") with the deadline pressure on his job. We defined his options as looking for another job or accepting the standards of his job and redefining the acceptability of work that was "less than his best."

When confronted with this deadline situation, his automatic thought was often: "I should be working elsewhere." He defined his goal as "to stay where I am and find a way not to drive myself crazy." He kept a log of situations, feelings, and thoughts, and quickly detected a pattern of anxiety–associated self–statements. After learning and rehearsing a series of "rational" responses, he noted that his anxiety symptoms diminished. Two months (six sessions) after we began, abdominal pain, sleep problems, headaches, blood pressure, and perceived anxiety were all diminished.

When I saw Mr. B. one month later in follow-up, we reviewed his complaints, how we had conceptualized the problem, the method applied, and the results. He had spoken to and believed that he had impressed his boss with the need to allow him to complete his work, when that was practical. He was better able to accept "the best he could do" when a deadline did not permit optimal work. He suggested to management that they consult him prior to signing the contract agreement specifying the date that the work was due. In this way, his input could be incorporated "before the fact." In his own way, then, he had achieved some needed control in a situation hitherto thought to be uncontrollable.

He believed that he had learned some things of value in therapy. He stated that he would return "only if the old symptoms came back and he couldn't walk through the method by himself." His final statement summarized for me the worth in treating this kind of problem. "In everyone's mailbox," he said, "there is space for a variety of service people: physician, lawyer, dentist, accountant. I can now add psychotherapist to that list. Thanks."

Ms. C. $\overline{\quad 15}$

The meaning of anxiety changed considerably between the publication of the American Psychiatric Association's *Diagnostic and Statistical Manual I*[33] in 1952 and *III*[34] in 1980. Originally discussed under the heading "Psychoneurotic Disorders," anxiety was defined in DSM–I as a characteristic "which may be felt and expressed or which may be unconsciously and automatically controlled by the utilization of various psychological defense mechanisms . . . [it is] a danger signal felt and perceived by the conscious portion of the personality. It is produced by a threat from within the personality" (p. 31). Three decades later, there is no longer any definition provided. Etiological (and theoretical) considerations are absent from DSM–III and its revision, DSM–III–R[35]. Instead, we have an impressive range of diagnostic entities, all related to anxiety: panic disorder, agoraphobia, social phobia, simple phobia, obsessive–compulsive disorder, post–traumatic stress disorder, and generalized anxiety disorder.

As we enter the decade of the nineties, many of these disorders (panic disorder, agoraphobia, obsessive–compulsive disorder) are being approached chemotherapeutically, suggesting a biological component. Each of these clinical entities related to anxiety has been treated with behavior modification, as well. And, while the cognitive model had its origins in the attempt to understand depression, Beck had developed a detailed approach to the anxiety disorders by the mid–1980s. His book[5] is replete with case anecdotes, excerpts, and examples.

It seems appropriate, therefore, to conclude this *Practical Guide* with a reminder that anxiety disorders respond to cognitive therapy approaches. I met this patient, Ms. C., several years before the publication of DSM–III. She had suffered symptoms of anxiety for three years before consulting a therapist. She was now in her middle twenties.

She described her condition as follows: "I often feel panicky," she said. "It's like there is a haze between me and other people. I worry about 'going off the deep end.' I feel trapped within my own body. I fear losing control of myself. Sometimes, I feel nothing. Ten days ago, I had difficulty breathing for the first time. I couldn't lie flat. I felt as if I was floating. I had the thought that I had died. This experience led me to finally call you up."

Over her 25 years, she had moved frequently, living in six different states. She had an older sister with anxiety problems and a father who had been depressed. He was distant, gruff and rarely home, always at work. Mother was more available, but overly controlling and rigid. She saw neither parent as a good role model for herself. Her sister had several times run away from home and now had a serious drug abuse problem.

After college, she had worked for a master's degree in English. She anticipated a career in creative writing, with financial support initially coming from a part-time job. Writing was, for her, "the most intimate thing." She met her husband while in college, and they were married three years before she came for therapy.

She described her goals for therapy as follows:

1. To become less afraid.
2. To be more assertive.
3. To avoid being like mother.
4. To be comfortable with success.

The working diagnosis was anxiety reaction (now, generalized anxiety disorder).

She used language carefully and it became clear early in therapy that I would have to be similarly precise in discussing concepts with her. There remained much identity formation to be done. A real separation from her family of origin had not been achieved, despite her marriage.

This cognitive therapy had little structure: no focus on automatic thoughts, no identification of cognitive errors or schemas. There were no formal triple columns and no homework. This psychotherapy was cognitive "in style." She would spend a session describing events and feelings. I would direct her to consider meanings and her thinking.

She discussed her marriage in detail and painted a picture of feeling trapped. Where she was impressionistic, he was precise. When she needed affection, he demanded distance. While she liked to think her way through problems, he needed to act quickly. While she chose fantasy as her constant companion, he remained dominated by a need for structure and reality.

Ms. C. considered leaving him and confronted how dependent she had become on his presence. In the process, she sketched an identity of who she wanted to be. She became more demanding of herself. She consulted a lawyer to learn the parameters of separation. She began to read poetry each night.

Over our initial 10 sessions, she began to grieve the anticipated loss of her husband. When she became aware that her parents too were considering divorce, she was for a time adrift without an anchor. Slowly, she accepted the realization that stability would mean more and more self-reliance. At times she got "hard on herself." She dropped her husband's name and resumed using her family name.

She began expressing her feelings in writing. She would bring in brief essays and we would read them together. We searched for clues to her thinking. When she expressed distress connected to a meaning, we looked together for alternatives. She developed the capacity to carry on this process, outside of therapy, by herself. "I don't want to deal with things forever by bringing them to my shrink," she said.

At the end of 15 sessions (four months), the frequency of anxiety symptoms had markedly decreased. When they occurred, she followed a predetermined sequence:

1. Label the reaction as "anxiety."
2. Locate the dominant problem or situation.
3. Search for the relevant cognition.
4. Think of as many alternative views as you can.

For me, it was the forerunner to a more structured "orthodox" cognitive therapy. For her, it was a logical way to approach a set of uncomfortable feelings that would lead to mastery and relief.

She found an apartment for herself. After signing a separation agreement, she considered how much her husband had "influenced her work." She thought more often now in terms of choices and consequences, working hard to accept responsibility for herself. Simultaneously, she felt that she had become the focal point for her family's problems. Separately, her mother, father, and sister had sought her out to help them with current difficulties. Ms. C. felt simultaneously abandoned (*she* had no family member to talk to) and overburdened (by the needs of her family).

More contact with mother seemed to validate her fear that she would turn out to be like her. It made some of her anxiety reactions understandable. At one point, she became extremely angry with mother and told her some things she had held back for many years. This brought her some relief, surprisingly little guilt, and a new basis for relating to her mother, who responded with some understanding and support.

By now, six months into therapy, a few of her discrete fears (of the dark, of being alone) had melted away. "I feel like I'm rearranging myself," she said. "I feel like I'm in transit." At the same time, her low tolerance for feeling anxious was giving way to understanding. It was okay now to occasionally "feel uptight." She saw much more of her world as under her control.

At this point, she brought in an unfinished, lengthy poem that we studied in detail. "I am happier and more comfortable than I have ever been," she said. "I'm also really proud of myself for what I have been able to achieve."

We terminated after eight months of therapy and had two follow-up sessions at six-month intervals. "All the things I'm discovering about myself have always been there," she said. "I let you see more of me than I ever have with a man in your age bracket. And you stayed friendly. I'm glad we worked together."

REFERENCES

1. Frank, J. D. (1974). *Persuasion and healing: A comparative study of psychotherapy.* New York: Schocken.
2. Orne, M. & Wender, P. (1968). Anticipatory socialization for psychotherapy: Method and rationale. *American Journal of Psychiatry, 124,* 1202-1211.
3. Watzlawick, P., Weakland, J. & Fisch, R. (1974). *Change: Principles of problem formation and problem resolution.* New York: Norton.
4. Beck, A. T., Rush, A. J., Shaw, B. F. & Emery, G. (1979). *Cognitive therapy of depression.* New York: Guilford.
5. Beck, A. T., Emery, G. & Greenberg, R. (1985). *Anxiety disorders and phobias: A cognitive perspective.* New York: Basic Books.
6. Sank, L. I. & Shaffer, C. (1984). *A therapist's manual for cognitive behavior therapy in groups.* New York: Plenum.
7. Perris, C. (1989). *Cognitive therapy with schizophrenic patients.* New York: Guilford.
8. Emery, G., Hollon, S. D. & Bedrosian, R. C. (1981). *New directions in cognitive therapy.* New York: Guilford.
9. Beck, A. T. (1988). *Love is never enough.* New York: Harper & Row.
10. Budman, S. (1985). *Forms of brief psychotherapy.* New York: Guilford.
11. Erikson, E. H. (1963). *Childhood and society.* New York: Norton.
12. Wolpe, J. (1958). *Psychotherapy by reciprocal inhibition.* Stanford: Stanford University Press.
13. Klerman, G. L., Weissman, M. M., Rounsaville, B. J. & Chevron, E. S. (1984). *Interpersonal psychotherapy of depression.* New York: Basic Books.
14. Sifneos, P. (1972). *Short-term psychotherapy and emotional crisis.* Cambridge, MA: Harvard University Press.
15. Mann, J. (1973). *Time-limited psychotherapy.* Cambridge, MA: Harvard University Press.
16. Malan, D. H. (1963). *A study of brief psychotherapy.* New York: Plenum.
17. Davanloo, H. (1976). *Basic principles and techniques in short-term dynamic psychotherapy.* New York: S. P. Medical & Scientific Books.
18. Mahoney, M. (1974). *Cognition and behavior modification.* Cambridge, MA: Ballinger.
19. Meichenbaum, D. (1977). *Cognitive-behavior modification.* New York: Plenum.
20. Ellis, A. (1962). *Reason and emotion in psychotherapy.* New York: Lyle Stuart.
21. Dobson, K. S. (1988). *Handbook of cognitive-behavioral therapies.* New York: Guilford.
22. Beck, A. T. (1976). *Cognitive therapy and the emotional disorders.* New York: International Universities Press.
23. Beck, A. T. (1961). A systematic investigation of depression. *Comprehensive Psychiatry, 2,* 163-170.

24. Beck, A. T. (1963). Thinking and depression. *Archives of General Psychiatry, 9,* 324–333.
25. Beck, A. T. (1967). *Depression: clinical, experimental and theoretical aspects.* New York: Harper & Row.
26. Meichenbaum, D. (1974). *Cognitive-behavioral modification: An integrative approach.* Morristown, NJ: General Learning Press.
27. Simons, A. D., Garfield, S. L. & Murphy, G. E. (1984). The process of change in cognitive therapy and pharmacotherapy for depression. *Archives of General Psychiatry, 41,* 45–51.
28. Hoehn-Saric, R., Liberman, B., Imber, S. D., Stone, A. R., Pande, S. K., & Frank, J. D. (1972). Arousal and attitude change in neurotic patients. *Archives of General Psychiatry, 26,* 51–56.
29. Burns, D. D. (1980). *Feeling good: The new mood therapy.* New York: William Morrow.
30. Viscott, D. (1977). *Risking.* New York: Simon & Schuster.
31. Bach, R. (1979). *Illusions: Confessions of a reluctant messiah.* New York: Dell.
32. Kopp, S. (1979). *What took you so long? An assortment of life's every-day ironies.* Palo Alto: Science and Behavior Books.
33. American Psychiatric Association. (1952). *Diagnostic and statistical manual.* Washington, DC: Author.
34. American Psychiatric Association. (1980). *Diagnostic and statistical manual III.* Washington, DC: Author.
35. American Psychiatric Association. (1987). *Diagnostic and statistical manual III-R.* Washington, DC: Author.

A COGNITIVE THERAPY
READING LIST

1. Beck, A. T. (1979). *Cognitive therapy and the emotional disorders.* New York: New American Library.
2. Burns, D. D. (1980). *Feeling good: The new mood therapy.* New York: New American Library.
3. Beck, A. T., Rush, A. J., Shaw, B. F. & Emery, G. (1979). *Cognitive therapy of depression.* New York: Guilford.
4. Beck, A. T., Emery, G. & Greenberg, R. (1985). *Anxiety disorders and phobias: A cognitive perspective.* New York: Basic.
5. Emery, G., Hollon, S. & Bedrosian, R. (1981). *New directions in cognitive therapy.* New York: Guilford.
6. McMullin, R. E. (1986). *Handbook of cognitive therapy techniques.* New York: Norton.
7. Beck, A. T. (1988). *Love is never enough.* New York: Harper & Row.
8. Schuyler, D. (1973). Some theoretical origins and therapeutic implications. *International Mental Health Newsletter, 15,* 12–16.
9. Perris, C. (1989). *Cognitive therapy with schizophrenic patients.* New York: Guilford.
10. Guidano, V. F. & Liotti, G. (1983). *Cognitive processes and emotional disorders.* New York: Guilford.

INDEX